The Dark Eye in Africa

LAURENS VAN DER POST

For Jane Rose,
" Hamba Gashe "

The Dark Eye in Africa

From
Laurens van der Post

WILLIAM MORROW
& COMPANY, INC.
New York

To

David Stirling for practising what he
preaches in Africa, and to those of
all races and colours who are trying
to make Capricorn a true instrument
of reintegration in Africa.

Contents

"You know, Laurens, if we were not humble enough to see ourselves as instruments of *le bon Dieu,* we could not have the arrogance to do what we are trying to do in Africa."

(David Stirling to Laurens van der Post)

Introduction

Introduction

The original talk from which this book emerged was given, in 1954, out of a sense of the urgency of events in Africa and the world. I had just returned to Europe from a long journey through Africa, dismayed by the swift increase of tension in men and their societies in my native continent. In particular, I was perturbed by what appeared to me to be a fatal time-lag between peoples "thinking" and their "doing." At the numerous meetings which I was asked to address on the concept of a greater Africa with a true integration of its multi-racial population, I often used as my text: "It is always later than you think." It seems that either the right idea comes too late to produce the appropriate deed; or the deed is impatient of the idea which alone can make it an instrument of life. It is as if between the imagination of men and their behaviour there is a gap through which evil and disaster drive. And it was this aspect of the African scene which perturbed me most. I had observed it too, at other times and places, particularly in Indonesia immediately after the last war, and this book shows how much I drew on my Indonesian experience.

To me it was a truly surprising and frightening thing that the Dutch, an admirable nation, able, industrious, enterprising and civilised, could rule and live on daily terms of intimacy for 350 years with the peoples of Indonesia and yet remain utterly unaware of the resentments they were piling up against themselves. This form of insensitivity of rulers to the ruled, this imperviousness of the powerful to the feelings and aspirations of the powerless, this failure of the imagination truly to preside over human conduct seemed to me one explanation of the fatal time-lag I have mentioned. Yet great as was this imperviousness of the European in the East it seemed little in comparison with what I had experienced in Africa.

The clearest example of this imperviousness again came from my Indonesian experience. There was one moment immediately after the Japanese surrender when the peoples of Indonesia were ready to forget and forgive their past and enter into a new relationship with their former rulers. I have not time here to describe it in detail. I can only say it was one of those rare instances in history when great opportunities are born: what one might call "a moment of innocence" occurred. Convinced of the immense opportunity of the new-born moment, I had been sent by my imaginative commander-in-chief, Lord Mountbatten, to consult with the British Cabinet in London. The British Prime Minister sent me to The Hague to talk to the Dutch Cabinet and despite the obvious reservations encountered, I returned to London convinced that the people of the Netherlands should be persuaded to recognise the moment and make the imaginative gesture to their Indonesian subjects which alone could bring them together in a more contemporary and creative relationship than in the past.

The night before I returned to Java, saying goodbye to the Vice Chief-of-the-Imperial Staff in London he asked me if I really thought this could be achieved. When I answered in the affirmative he replied: "I wish I could think so too. But history teaches me that human beings always give too little and too late. Then under pressure they give reluctantly bit by bit until in the end they have given far more than was originally necessary or even asked for, only to find that even that much is no longer enough. But don't let that prevent you from having a good try."

We did indeed have a good, long try at it, and failed. As a result the Dutch have vanished for all practical purposes from those islands—though in the end under pressure they had to give more than was originally necessary. The failure was all the more tragic because they and the Indonesians had need of one another and a common experience which, if imaginatively reappraised, could have enriched their lives together whereas today, in isolation and estrangement, they are both the poorer. Yet still I remain convinced that this need not have been. If the Dutch at the moment of which I have spoken had offered the Indonesians the equivalent of British Commonwealth Dominion Status they would have grasped it warmly with both hands. But sadly there was this gap between their imagination and behaviour which produced a time-lag that was fatal.

How, I asked myself in 1954, could we prevent a similar fate in Africa where this imperviousness went far deeper than even in the East? I was cer-

tain there could be no answer to the question unless one uncovered the fundamental reason for the
split between the spirit and the actions of men.
The part which history, economics, colour and racial
prejudices played in the tensions increasing with
geometric progression in Africa was clear enough.
But even in unison I could not feel them to amount
to a first cause. There was something else which
went far deeper, and I believed it was only by trying to discover what that was that men could acquire a capacity for preventing a repetition of the
most discredited aspects of life.

This book was my own diffident attempt to un-
cover the first cause of negation and disaster in
Africa. I could add a great deal to it today. And if
I wrote it now I would do so with an even greater
sense of urgency. If it was later than we thought
then, how much later is it not now? Already we
have had a more contemporary echo of the Dutch
cry of astonishment in the East in the outraged
Belgian surprise in the Congo. In Central Africa
unrest and confusion have grown, rioting become
more frequent, and in my native South Africa the
white rulers of the land resort daily to more repres-
sive, shameful and out-worn methods. There is in

Africa little left of "the moment of innocence." Yet there is still, I believe, just enough of it to make rebirth possible. So although I would qualify some things in this book and enlarge on others, I would not alter it greatly because the basic proposition seems to me valid. I believe more than ever that if the world is to prevent endless recurrence of the cataclysms of the past, different only in the widening scale of their effect and horror, it must set before all other tasks the achievement of the greater kind of awareness after which this book gropes. The battle for Africa, for the peace and the sanity of men which in its ancient sense meant wholeness of mind and body, the spirit made immediate in being, is so urgent that it has to be fought on all levels of life; national, international, economic, ideologic, political, artistic and spiritual. But it can be fought successfully only if the individual carries with him an awareness within himself of the forces and values discussed here.

I would say that the gravest threat to the democratic way of life comes not from some totalitarian power from without, but from this failure to recognise the importance of the imponderable beginnings of great events. Democracy is so organised that it experiences no concern for situations until they have acquired bulk and pressure. By then they are already difficult, if not perilous, to handle. They have in fact, like the post-war situation in the East or the present one in the Congo, lost their innocence, and acquired a character, will and negative history of their own. Through neglect and lack of affection from the established order, they have become, in fact, ugly delinquent children of history. As a result there seem to be as many delinquents let loose on the international scene as there are at night in the back streets of London.

This failure has come about, I believe, through the failure of the individual to recognise the importance of first things in himself. Men cannot achieve publicly what they have not accomplished within the private bounds of their own personality. The future, thus, depends much on the speed with which the individual can achieve this greater awareness and the degree to which his life is lived in obedience to it.

Finally I am asked repeatedly by friends and readers in America: what of Capricorn and its founder to whom this book is dedicated?

Since David Stirling first founded the Capricorn

Africa Society some eleven years ago, and I joined in the task, it has suffered many adversities and achieved many triumphs. At the moment membership, in comparison with the vast numbers who flock round the standards of racialists and extremists in Africa, could be written off as negligible. But the object of the society has never been to attract a vast membership. Its aim was to make black, coloured and white persons *aware* of the dangerous inadequacies of the established order—to plan and work together for a greater Africa free of all crippling obsessions with race and colour. The various ways in which David Stirling and Capricorn set about this task need the book which he is about to write. But here are a few examples of what they have accomplished.

First, there was the drawing up of the Capricorn Charter and a Bill of Rights for contemporary man in Africa. Citizenship committees were set up all over British Africa and for some years worked at formulating the basic principles on which a new society free of race, colour and religious discrimination could be set up and safeguarded. All these proposals were pooled and laid before a great convention at Salima on Lake Nyasa some four years ago.

Introduction

It was the first occasion on which black, coloured, white and Asian from all over Africa met to devise a common plan for their greater destiny. To this day the people who were there are still spurred on by the memory of the real breakthrough that the convention accomplished. Even African leaders who have never been members of Capricorn have tapped the contents of the Capricon Charter for their own programmes. Perhaps the most striking example has been the evolution of Tanganyika. Capricorn did not function there directly except briefly in the beginning in order to launch a movement on parallel lines. The happy issue of events in Tanganyika (which is an example to the rest of Africa) would have been inconceivable without the precept and the leaven of Capricorn philosophy. Even the latest proposition of Tanganyika's chief minister, Mr. Jules Nyerere, for a greater Federation of Tanganyika, Kenya, Uganda, the Rhodesias and Nyasaland was first conceived and advocated by Capricorn. That to my mind is one of the great achievements of Capricorn. For the various peoples of Africa it gave expression to their immense challenge in terms that no one could ignore. In arguing for or against its concepts they clarified their own vision of the future, with the result that men and women in Africa think today in a manner they could not have done if Capricorn had not existed. Indeed, Capricorn was the first attempt made on African soil to evolve a contemporary political philosophy not just for a special race, privileged caste or territory but for a whole continent. And the evolution continues. Wherever the re-examination of our constitutions and social systems in British Africa take place and new instruments of change are being forged, Capricorn is there to urge out of its most recent experience its own version of the future.

Again Capricorn realised from the start that this greater Africa could not come about except by a process of profound re-education of all the peoples in Africa. So it became the instrument for founding the Colleges of Citizenship working to that end today in East Africa and Rhodesia. In London it brought about the establishment of a home where students of all the races and colours from Africa are housed under a single roof. The home is called Zebra House after Capricorn's heraldic emblem, which was chosen originally because it represents an animal both black and white. Already the accommodation has had to be doubled and, small as it is, it is one of the most inspiring institutions of its kind in Britain.

Other examples abound from the specific to the general. The battle fought and won in Southern Rhodesia to change the law so that a Rhodesian African called to the bar in London could return to practice his chosen profession in his native country; the formation of political parties in East and Central Africa to fight the Capricorn battle. But perhaps most important of all has been the example set by individual members of Capricorn. They were the first to travel the land with black, coloured and Asian colleagues sharing the same accommodations and appearing on the same platforms to speak on a common issue. I have often been warmed by the welcome which our white hostesses have given to my black companions on these journeys, and by the way in which they have tried to live their lives in the challenging context of Africa without colour prejudice. The hotels in Kenya today no longer have a colour bar. The schools are being opened to children of all races. And the land on the White Highlands, for so long an exclusive settler fortress, is now made available also to African farmers. All these things have come about largely because they were local Capricorn targets.

Finally the "success" or "lack of success" of Capricorn to me is not the matter of primary importance. In any case one man's lifetime is too short to be able to judge accurately of such matters. But we have helped to push events in the right direction and what more could one ask of life?

Not long ago a priest on the borders of the Congo said to me in despair: "What you're doing is no use. We're in for a period of disaster in Africa and must reconcile ourselves to the fact."

I answered: "I don't believe that it is so. But supposing you're right, it is still a point of honour to do everything possible to prevent such a disaster if only to make certain that when it comes it may turn out to be the right sort of disaster."

I myself have no doubt that Capricorn has been an instrument in the world of the immediacy of man's timeless search for greater awareness as discussed in this book and in the process diminished this time-lag I mentioned at the beginning.

LAURENS VAN DER POST

London, November 1960

Introduction (1954)

Originally I gave this talk and answered some of the questions, of which this book is made up, at a combined meeting of the C. J. Jung Institute and the Psychological Club of Zurich in March, 1954. I repeated the talk on other occasions elsewhere in Europe and in England, where I was asked more questions and gave more answers, some of which are also included in this book. The original title was "Mata Kelap, or the Appearance of the Dark Eye in Africa: A Talk on the Invisible Origins of African Unrest." I gave the talk at all times and at all places with considerable diffidence. I thought there was some danger that I might merely add to the confusion in a field of trouble which, God knows, is dark and confused enough. I was persuaded, however, to speak because it was felt that since I was born in Africa I could talk of it out of the experience of my own mind and spirit, and that that perhaps would add to the understanding of the problem.

Later, when I came to consider the question of publication I was even more diffident. In Zurich any confusion I might have caused was discounted in advance by the fact that I was speaking to a specialized audience who had their own technique for separating the wheat from the chaff. But these safeguards were not likely to exist when the published book was available to any curious reader. However, I decided to agree to publication out of a profound conviction that sooner or later something akin to my talk must be put before my countrymen, and all those who are interested in Africa, if this terrible conflict in which they are engaged is ever to be resolved without disaster.

Nothing describes the origin of things more authoritatively and movingly for me than the description in Genesis. First, there is the spirit moving ceaselessly over the great and formless waters of time in search of flesh and blood to give it life and reality. Then there comes the *Word*. That is the great opening phrase which falls on our dreaming senses like a trumpet call to battle. I feel convinced that before a new spirit can come to painful birth in this terrible conflict in Africa and find true and just expression in a new form of society and human reality, there has first to be the word to give it form and expression—a means of communication. If, therefore, people like myself who have experienced this conflict, who feel deeply about it and who believe that it need not end in retrograde disaster but can be a new and tremendous achievement for the spirit of Western man, if we hesitate to put forward our suggestions as to what this dynamic key word may be, then the battle could be lost before it was even joined.

And therein, perhaps, lies one of the most profound problems of our time. The human spirit is being served by words, ideas, and world concepts that have become totally inadequate for the meaning which it is trying to express and the being which it is trying to create. I believe that of all the means which man uses to win his way through life with dignity and honour, the spirit of man and the ideas by which that spirit expresses itself are by far the most important. But in this age of shallow extrovert rationalism, this aspect of life is the most neglected, and in the greatest need of repair. I believe one of the reasons why Western man has been failing in increasing measure in his contacts all over the world is because the ideas by which his spirit expresses itself are no longer contemporary. They need to be de-conditioned from associations that do not belong to our age, and to be reassessed in terms of our own living experience in its fullest contemporary meaning. Further, I believe that the ideas that we use and on which we base our actions are unworthy of the being which is clamouring for expression in modern man. It is the bigoted rationalism and fanatic adherence of Western man to outer physical reality and his overvaluation of the demonstrable objective world round him which is the cause of much of his undoing. He is neglecting all manner of invisible and imponderable values in his own life, and therefore ignoring them in the lives of those in his power, or in the lives of those with whom he is thrown into contact. Those factors sooner or later combine in rebellion against him. The explosions which are blowing European man out of so many parts of the world and which are making many so-called inferior, less cultured and less civilized nations increasingly mistrustful of him, are caused largely by his neglect of these great imponderables in himself—and therefore inevitably in others. This is particularly true of Africa. Africa demonstrates this failure in its most dramatic and tangible form. But I realize that so far as Africa is concerned the solution has to come out of Africa itself and can no longer come directly from Europe. I think the right solution anywhere can only come out of the lives of the people who have to live the solution, and cannot be thought out for them by others.

In this book I speak of the European man in Africa but I realize it is an inadequate term. I would rather talk of "Africans, black, white and coloured," * for the older I grow the more I realize how inaccurate it is to think of the white man in Africa as a European. Even I, whose father was born in Europe, realize how inadequate it is for me to think of myself as a European. Consciously there is a part of me that is closely identified with Europe, but at heart I am indelibly and irrevocably in and of Africa. I realize it in the smallest details of my thinking and in the most sensitive responses of my nature. Much as I love Europe, I am continually being reminded that the master pattern at work within me, the magnet which conditions the field of all my reactions, is African. I have, even in the midst of the greyest

* In Africa the word "coloured" is used to designate people of mixed blood.

winter day in the streets of London, found my eyes dazzled by some inward glance at the Africa which forever I carry about within me. But between this love of Europe and this sense of Africa I feel myself to have become a kind of improvised footbridge across the widening chasm between Europe and Africa, and this alone perhaps is justification for this book.

There is, too, a deeper and wider consideration which helped me to make the decision. I believe the problem in Africa to be fundamentally a problem of *being*, both in the nature and character of those in command of the situation. I know the problem in Africa can be studied in a variety of ways, economically, historically, scientifically, anthropologically and sociologically. These are all perfectly valid ways of investigation, and none of them lacks impassioned advocates. But I see them as approaches of secondary not primary importance. For me the one primary and elemental approach to the problem is through the being of man. Unfortunately it is an increasingly lonely way, trodden more and more not by masses but by solitary individuals, or as Nietzsche might have said, "Only by hermits and hermits in pairs." In the past it was a way which was primarily the concern of the churches, but today so many of the churches themselves seem to have lost the way. One of the most terrible phenomena of our time is the failure of the churches almost everywhere to keep alive man's natural sense of religion and to sustain his urge to seek an answer to the riddle of life through the quality and temper of his being. So another and more sinister dimension has been added to our failure in Africa, for there the churches of my own people seem to me to be actually standing between man and this ancient, respected way. This is what I would call "sabotage in the fourth dimension." This breakdown in man's traditional machinery for dealing with the kind of problem and conflict which confronts him in Africa today means that the task can now be helped only by those individuals who are aware of this failure. No matter how inadequate our spirit and talents may seem, we must all, out of our experience and intuitions, try to act as footbridges in order to breach this terrible gulf between ourselves and our own people. For I am convinced that there is no solution for the conflict in Africa, or in the world, unless there is first of all a change in the heart and understanding of man, and I do not see how that change of heart can come about until the white man in Africa starts to think about himself in a new way. Therefore what I publish here is merely how one African, with the pattern of Africa very deep within him, has conceived that some of the conditions of this new thinking might be brought about. I put them forward not as a proud absolute but as a humble relative; I speak not as a teacher but as one of the guinea pigs in this vast laboratory of our time.

In view of this ominous breakdown in the religious machinery in Africa, writers—both in Africa and of Africa—have a tremendous responsibility laid upon them. Art to me is the technique of presenting unrealized and hidden values to people potentially capable of appreciating and understanding those values. It is a vehicle in which men can penetrate places in their minds and souls that they had never reached before. Writing especially can be a kind of magic mirror which holds up to man and society the neglected and unrealized aspects of himself and his age. Writing can be many other things as well, but at this desperate moment I think this may be its most important function. Particularly is this true of Africa. I believe that if we are to come without disaster through the conflict which confronts us, those

who write of Africa and those who write in Africa
must never for a minute forget to hold up this magic
mirror before both their and our eyes. Indeed, the
cause in South Africa, in particular, almost certainly
will be lost if the writer in Afrikaans does not join
the South African writers in English who are trying
to do this very thing. The communities of my Afrikaner countrymen are becoming more and more iso-
lated from their time and from the contemporary
spirit of the world. There is an immense tract of experience to which they deny a place in their awareness. Perhaps this is one of the reasons why this
blight has fallen upon the literature of my country. I
have noticed that when my fellow-writers in Afrikaans first start writing as young people immediately
concerned with the instinctive and lyrical issues of
youth, they write superbly in a manner which can
be compared with the literature of the world. However, very few of them seem to be able to carry this
great gift through with them into maturity, and I
am certain that this is largely because there is an
issue which they are shirking in their own awareness. There is a reality in their lives which they refuse to accept and include in their values. If you

read the literature of my Afrikaner countrymen, you
will be amazed to find that a people who are thrown
daily into contact with the black and coloured man,
and who have been in close and intimate contact
with him not only for days and years but for generations, in their literature show no awareness of him
as a human being. In their writing he does not exist
as an individual with his own unique being and individual claims. He exists, perhaps, as a generalized
function, a servant in a comical, villainous or prob-
lematical role. But as a rounded human being in his
own individual right he is as absent as the English
workingman of the eighteenth century was from a
tea-party of Miss Austen's young ladies. Further,
when you consider that most Afrikaner writers, like
myself, had black nurses beside their cradles, black
play-fellows and black servants interwoven into all
the magical and living tapestry of their childhood,
when you consider that the master moments of their
early lives and imaginations were lived in the intimate company of these black people, and when you
then discover that they are as readily excluded from
the understanding and imagination of the grown-up
Afrikaner as are the black and coloured people from
the justice and the love of his society, you will real-

ize what a terrible crippling of the human spirit and
what a maiming of the artist this must be.

I therefore publish this also as an appeal to my
Afrikaner countrymen in our great and inspiring
country. I beg all those individuals in Africa who,
like me, differ with their communities in their attitude towards the black and coloured people of
Africa, to stand fast in those differences, and live
them out, no matter what it costs. The individual
everywhere owes it to his community always to dis-
own the renegade aspects of that community. The
Afrikaans writer can no longer pretend that he is
unaware of the behaviour of his people. They, his
people, may not know what they are doing, but he,
the artist, surely must know by now. He must know
that what we are doing to the black and coloured
people in Africa is dishonourable and evil. He cannot continue sinking his own individual standards
to the level of a debased herd-instinct. He cannot go
on hiding behind the degrading morality of his nation in its treatment of its black and coloured people.
If he has any pretensions to being an artist and an
individual, he must throw off the anthropoidal concepts of his nation and walk upright in a morality
of his own. What is more, he must do this if he wants

his own people to survive; and his own people will only survive if he helps them to change their hearts *now,* for already it is later than most of us realize.

To my black and coloured countrymen who may read this book I would like to explain my use of the words "primitive" and "civilized" man. I use these words only because I know no others to denote the general difference of being which undeniably exists between indigenous and European man in Africa. I am, however, fully conscious of their limitations and relativity. They are not intended to convey a feeling of superiority. I do not think of the European as a being superior to the black man. I think of both as being different and of the differences as honourable differences equal before God. The more I know of "primitive" man in Africa the more I respect him and the more I realize how much and how profoundly we must learn from him. I believe our need of him is as great as his is of us. I see us as two halves designed by life to make a whole. In fact, as I watch the darkening scene, I see this need of one for the other to be so great as to create fresh hope that this very need may yet save Africa from disaster, if nothing else will. We need the good that is in the values of "primitive" man in Africa. Vast arid stretches in

our own bigoted culture can be made fertile again
by opening our culture to his urgent awakening
spirit. Between us I believe we can make civilization greater and life richer on earth than it has ever
been. For this reason I wish we could stop thinking
about the difficulties and perils of the encounter
of white and black in Africa, and instead commit
our hearts and imaginations to this rich and immeas-
urable opportunity it presents to both of us. I believe there has never before been such an opportunity in the history of man. Could we but see—white
and black—how lucky we are to have found each
other at this far crossroad in time, half the battle for
Africa, as I call it to myself, would be won. It is this
which makes the effort of my countrymen to exclude
the black and coloured man from society so profoundly ironic and tragic. We force the African continually to take from us and prevent him from giving
to us in his own rich way; we deny Africa its own
unique creativeness. It is this frustration which is
inflaming "primitive" man in Africa in the individual
as well as the collective sense. Nor am I unaware,
when I speak of "primitive" man, that there are
thousands of black people in Africa who are as
"civilized" as any of us. Like me and many others of

my white countrymen, those thousands are the permanently de-tribalized children of Africa. I know from my own experience how terrible is their frustration and how great their anguish of spirit and mind. But I know, too, that bitterness departs from suffering when one finds out the meaning of that suffering, and I hope that what I write here may perhaps put some de-tribalized heart on the way to finding a meaning in what it is so grimly asked to endure. If it can learn to see itself as the privileged seedbed of the greater Africa to come, if it can see its suffering as a commitment in a great cause of life, if it can realize also that there are many white persons who are already joined with it in the same living cause of the greater Africa, some of the bitterness may fall away. This bitterness is our mutual enemy and the enemy of the community to come. Above all I think of this in connection with the great coloured community of the Cape of Good Hope. I feel even more deeply the shame of what we are doing to them. They are of our own blood and creation. They speak our own tongue and share our religion. They have enriched the music, humour and spirit of the Afrikaner. They, too, participated and suffered in as great a measure as our ancestors did on their hazardous thrust into the interior of Africa. They have earned a right also to be their changing and greater selves. Indeed, the general injustice of our attitude to non-European Africa is made grimmer by what I feel to be a conscious act of deliberate betrayal. Their temptation to bitterness must be the most powerful of all, and yet they, too, have to hold out against it if this greater nonracial Africa is to come.

One last word about the form of this book. What I want to convey is not advocacy or a reasoned statement of a rational case. I have tried to present a more complete and immediate aspect which did not exclude the rational but which included the "great imponderables." I have tried to speak from what I regard as the centre of myself, from a point in total awareness where my experience of the past and my intuition of the future, where my conscious knowledge of life, Africa, the world, and my own urgent feeling about them, meet. If it can be read also from the reader's centre, from a point where his sense of the past and the future, where both his knowledge and expectations of life meet, if it can be read with his heart as well as his mind, I shall not fear the result.

The Basis for Discussion

"Les lois fondamentales de l'esprit restent les mêmes, au moins pour les périodes historiques si courtes, dont nous avons connaissance; et presque tous les phénomènes, même les plus étranges, doivent pouvoir s'expliquer par ces lois communes de l'esprit que nous pouvons constater en nous-mêmes." *

Guillaume Ferrero

* The fundamental laws of the spirit remain the same, at least for the brief periods of history of which we have knowledge; and almost all phenomena, even the strangest, should be capable of explanation by those common laws of the spirit that we can observe in ourselves.

Dr. Meier, Dr. Jung, Ladies and Gentlemen, I have been encouraged by my recollection of the hearing you gave me here two years back to come and talk to you again about Africa. Once again I am not going to try to describe the great tide of unrest which is rising in Africa in terms of the inflated currency of conventional history and the fashionable idiom of economic materialism. For me the accepted concepts of this attitude have been worn so threadbare by frantic use that they barely conceal the thin and wasting shape, the skeleton beneath the taut skin of the mind and spirit of our day. Besides, if I did this I would produce an incomplete canvas with only its formal background sketched in and its real subject, its contemporary meaning, its inner significance here and now at 8:15 on the evening of March 3, 1954, completely absent. It would be like a performance of *Hamlet* with the role of the Prince of Denmark cut out of it. For a great deal of the trouble in Africa is due precisely to the fact that the people in command of the situation, the white ruling races, do ignore the inner realities of the situation, and do not seem to have even an inkling that what they are faced with is a problem, very largely, of great imponderables of being. This is what makes it so difficult for me to talk to most people in my country. I spend a great deal of my time in Africa, much of my work is centred there, and since there are great tracts of my imagination and physical and psychic energy which are inevitably at the disposal only of Africa, conversation should be easy. But it is not. I find it increasingly difficult, often impossible. I long passionately to talk and act on behalf of Africa, for I feel I have something I must say and an urgent warning of great and growing peril to convey. But often when I do so the same iron curtain that shuts many people off from the daily, recurring reality of their own lives cuts them off from the idiom necessary for understanding what the unrest in Africa is really about. It is as if, in conversation, one is forced to ape the unaware rulers of Africa and deal continually with a four dimensional reality through only two of its aspects, a process which invariably results in caricature. Worse still, the time is now upon us when almost anything said about Africa which is not violently partisan tends inevitably to be thought wrong and to give awful offence to both sides involved. Yet the two warring surface dimensions of the conflict in Africa are not the whole of the problem, any more than the white tip of ice sparkling brightly above the black water is the whole of the iceberg. However, I count myself lucky tonight in that I am faced with none of these difficulties, that I have not to define my definitions, that I can speak out freely and fully without fear of being misunderstood, my only obstacle being my own limitations.

Now what precisely is this unrest in Africa? I take it you all know of its existence, for the newspapers of the world devote much space and attention to it. In fact, the world's interest in this African unrest has about it such a singularly compelled quality that I shall presently have to return to examine it as a relevant factor. In the meanwhile, I hope you will allow me to take your knowledge of the unrest for granted and I will add only this: the physical Africa I am talking to you about tonight is the Africa south of the Sahara. The invisible spiritual Africa that is at stake has no frontiers and is as wide and deep as the human soul itself. In North Africa there is a great and growing unrest, too, but it is not what I would call specifically African unrest. Basically, in matter and spirit, North Africa is part of the old Mediterranean complex of the world with a heavy emphasis on the near eastern and Levantine ends. Even its flora and fauna are not African, but Mediterranean and European. The original, most ancient Africa stretching far, far back with unbelievable continuity to a time long before vegetable and animal life had being, to before the waters started to dream of fish and the fish of man—that Africa begins only south of the Sahara. And in this ancient Africa I am concerned principally with the British sections, not because what I have to say does not apply in varying degrees to the French, Belgian and Portuguese territories, but because the British section is by far the largest and most representative. Also, for reasons that are not necessarily discreditable to the British, this unrest which we have to consider is in these areas at its most advanced development. This immense tract of British Africa is divided administratively and politically into all sorts of sizes and shapes, condominiums, dominions, fed-

erations, unions, self-governing colonies, Crown
colonies and protectorates, with frontiers drawn
arbitrarily between them. But I do not propose going into those superficial differences and variations,
for these territories in their inner nature and reaction to life and time ignore physical differences and
political separation and are in reality and unfolding
purpose completely one. So, now to get back to my
original question. What precisely is this unrest in
Africa?

As I see it, there are at least four dimensions, four
levels of reality, wherein this unrest is germinated,
has its being, and wherein it increases alarmingly.
First of all there is a cosmic, universal dimension.
On that level I think of African unrest as unrest
which has its being in time. I wish I could be more
specific about this, but, alas, I have no knowledge of
any demonstrable proof or controlled research on
these lines to communicate to you. I can only offer
it as something which I apprehend intuitively, a
cinematographic image projected brilliantly from
the great darkness of unknowing around us onto the
brief screen of my mind. I know full well how
dangerous and unreliable these unsubstantiated
offerings can be. But I know also that often in war

and peace, in the bush and the desert in Africa when I have had only these hunches to steer by, with no objective knowledge of any kind to help me in my predicament, these intuitive apprehensions have served me greatly. They have saved my life more than once. Added to this, the older I grow the more I am convinced that there is something very wrong with our Western conception of time. I think we abuse and entirely misunderstand its meaning. Our Western conception of it is shallow and immature and some of our trouble may be directly due to our ignorance and neglect of time's full nature. For most of us time is only a "when," a linear current measured by the ticking of clocks over which it flows like water over a wheel, a measure completely at our disposal and according to which we make dates and keep our business appointments. We are so caught up in this linear movement that we never stop to consider that time may also have content and nature, a specific meaning of its own which makes it not merely a "when" but also a "what" and perhaps, more important still, also a "how" and a "way to eternity." I suggest, therefore, that incorporated somewhere in the inner pattern of misunderstood time there exists a blueprint from the master architect of life itself, a chart of the ultimate design of being which ceaselessly communicates to us our own unique share in time's fashioning according to the way our lives have to take shape. Or, if you like a more modern comparison, I believe there exists a kind of radar which, if we are properly tuned in, can bring us to our appropriate landing-ground through the thickest fogs and darknesses of existence. The moment we ignore this "what" and "how" of time and fail to build according to the original chart and blueprint of life, the moment we neglect to fly by this radar, then unrest, this searching, increasingly panicky unrest which is so characteristic of our day, invades our aboriginal hearts and minds and infects our behaviour, institutions and societies like a new black plague. I believe myself that at the moment there are indications on this inner blueprint which demand a change of direction in our course, a demand, however, of which the world is either unaware or towards which it is deliberately turning blind eyes and deaf ears. There is a kind of shrinking back, a profound fear and horror of being our 1954 selves. As a result, since whether we like it or not we are part of the time we live in, we are inflicted with this unrest not only publicly but also in the privacy of our lives and the silences of the night. So for what it is worth I give it you as my conviction that in the first place the unrest in Africa is part of an infinitely wide disquiet about the current trend of our life on this earth. On that level the unrest in Africa is universal unrest.

The second level I believe is global, as opposed to cosmic. On this level, though our canvas is still terrifyingly wide and large, we can speak with greater confidence and with less danger of being misunderstood. For though the invisible, dynamic, objective world that we carry about within us is so real to our inner senses, it is still held by some people to be an illusion, and so intuitive apprehensions of destiny and meaning are disregarded.* This much proof of it, however, is in our daily pudding of reality. No matter how much we may disagree about causes and origins, no matter which ideological recipe is our pet aversion or who is given the blame for the sticky

* I know it sounds paradoxical to speak of an inner objectivity. But for me the paradox is only apparent. Also, I believe that some of the worst confusions in contemporary thinking and doing arise from the general failure to realize that there is as great an "objective within" as there is an "objective without." The soul of man, for instance, is one such objective within and dreams are an objective manifestation within, since they exist in their own right and no man, however hard he tries, can determine what he shall dream. He can but be dreamed upon.

mess on our daily table, none of us can deny the disturbed and unpalatable state of the world we live in. Moreover, the pudding is not getting sweeter, nor the disturbance less. In fact, many of us feel this unrest like a sickness of the bowels, and so widespread and complex is it that I am hard put to talk of it in a few words for fear of oversimplification. However, I would suggest to you briefly that on the world level of international affairs this unrest expresses itself in a sense of conflict, physical and spiritual, among those races and groups who believe that they have been unfairly denied the opportunity of being themselves, and who now consequently fight back against the circumstances and people whom they blame for the long-sustained denial. Hence, for example, the insurgence of the peoples of the East against the West, particularly against those nations who have either invaded them directly or dominated them indirectly through trade and other external means since the sixteenth century. The rulers now are either on the defensive like the French in Indo-China, or evicted against their will like the Dutch from Indonesia, or voluntarily and honourably withdrawn like the British from Burma and India. This insurgent front in the old world shows an imposing battle-line of discontented, searching, bewildered and increasingly angry people, from Morocco right across to the great wall of that ancient land of China whose secret, wise old heart one might have hoped would have made it an exception to the sad general rule. There is resurgence, too, as spiritually active if not as dramatic, in the return of the vanished Indian world of Maya, Aztec and Inca, which is taking place in the New World. Look at their art and listen to their music and you will discern the stealthy step of sly, ancient, American spirits walking catfooted through the backdoors, cunning corridors, trap doors and endless catacombs of the human mind. But to sum up I would say that this conflict in the world is a struggle between the have-nots and the haves; between under-dog and top-dog; between under-culture and top-culture; between under-mind and top-mind, or, if you like, between unconsciousness and consciousness. In that dimension, I suggest to you, the unrest in Africa is a part of world unrest.

The third dimension wherein I think of the unrest in Africa is a European and more particularly a national British level. The struggle that has raged increasingly within the social framework of all nations since the French Revolution is, I am sure, as familiar to you as to me. There is no need for me to elaborate the general European theme for you. I would like to draw your attention only to one specific phenomenon in the general process because it illustrates a significant aspect of the problem we are discussing. When the excessively nationalist trend in French history reached its social climax in revolution, there was an official ceremony in Paris at which God was deposed and a goddess of reason crowned in His place. Just before that happened there emerged from the mind of a solitary Frenchman, Jean Jacques Rousseau, almost as if by spontaneous generation, the concept of "the noble savage" which has haunted the imagination of artists, poets and social reformers ever since. You have there, I believe, not only an example of how life preserves proportion and balance by continually going over into the opposites of its excesses, but also an indication of how profound and mysterious is the origin of the unrest we are discussing. On the surface it, too, is a struggle between those who want to conserve a certain pattern of society and those who want to change it. In Britain the conflict already has progressed so far that the class outline of the struggle has become blurred and I believe will soon disappear to leave the two protagonists, stripped of all rationalistic trappings and conscious justifications, exposed in their true colours as two partners; or better still, two opposite complementary principles, the one wanting to conserve and contain, the other wanting to break out and to change; in brief, a classic and a romantic urge. Man from birth, it seems, is forced to identify himself with one or other of these urges and is seldom capable of combining the two. It is significant that in the main the Conservative in Britain tends to side automatically with the white man in Africa, while the Socialist tends to identify himself automatically with the black man. But what is important to our discussion of African unrest is that automatically both these political divisions in British society project their own tensions and their own differences into Africa. It is inevitable that on the Western level and most particularly in this British dimension, I think of the unrest in Africa also as European unrest.

Last and by no means least there is a fourth dimension wherein the unrest in Africa is peculiarly African unrest. It is on this level primarily that I want to speak to you tonight, for it is the dimension that completes the square and gives contemporary meaning to all the others that I have mentioned.

I begin with Africa in the physical sense; I begin with the earth of Africa. Now, Africa is old in the longest measure of time on earth. It is old in a way which makes the lovely white mountains in Switzerland not solid immovable matter but waves curling and breaking in the storm of time, wherein even Everest is but the ghostly spume of spray torn by an angry gust from curling breakers. Long before vegetable, organic or biological matter were in being, the rocks and earth of Africa as we know them today were already formed. Indeed, those of us who are born in Africa are born with a sense of this old oldness deep within us. For Africa was once part of a vast land-continent to which geologists, with a touch of whimsicality unusual to their sober and austere kind, have given the name of Gondwanaland, a name which has an odd gone-with-the-wind nostalgia implicit in its sound. So vast was this continent that it included part of Brazil, the Deccan, Madagascar and Australia. When I first went to Australia, although at the time I did not know this geological fact, my senses told me at once that here, beyond rational explanation, was a land physi-

cally akin to Africa. You have only to look at the
great waters which separate Africa today from the
other fragments of Gondwana-land and, remember-
ing how slowly and patiently water nibbles away at
rock, you can get an idea of how incredibly old
Africa really is. In those far, remote days Africa
was separated from Europe by the great sea of
Tethys, but as this sea shrank and life appeared on
the newly formed coasts, as the sea-boards gradually
linked up into the pattern of earth that we know today and created everywhere opportunities of vast
interchanges of life and emerging cultures, Africa
was enabled by a miraculous design of nature to be
an exception to the general. Her coastline, no matter
how the sea nibbled at it, kept its defences intact
and, when it gave way, retreated in good Mace-
donian order. To this day the coastline of Africa not
only offers no convenient natural harbours but most
of it, together with the interior, is raised above the
water level and the rivers come tumbling out of it
in swift, churning, angry torrents that make naviga-
tion up these streams impossible. Where the earth
was not so raised this ancient land threw up vast
seas of desert which could be crossed only by a few
initiates at their peril. Also, as if to make quite sure

that her defences completely sealed Africa off from the outer world, nature developed the most redoubtable champions in the mosquito and tsetse fly and other minute parasites, all able to strike down any invader with a wonderful selection of deadly diseases, from sleeping sickness, malaria, dysentery and typhoid, to leprosy and bubonic plague. One day I hope to persuade my fellow-Africans to put up a monument to the despised mosquito and tsetse fly for discharging so well this task of defending Africa against invasion. Just another example, one might think, of the way in which destiny so often selects its most significant instruments from the humble, drab and inconspicuous, no matter whether they be merely tsetse flies and mosquitoes, or peasant girls and house-painters!

So in this way Africa was enabled, undisturbed, to develop its own forms of life and its own nature on an infinitely richer and more varied scale than any other continent. I wish I could show you this miracle of Africa, instead of merely talking about it, for even today there are large sections of it which are as they have always been, immense tracts whose people still observe their traditional ways in another and more ancient dimension of time. There are still primeval territories, scenes of unexploited mountain and lake, river, plain and forest, and patterns of animal life that you see nowhere else in the world. For instance, there are more than one hundred and thirty kinds of lovely, bounding antelope in Africa which are unknown anywhere else in the world. No country ever had such varieties of life, from the most minute viruses and microbes, insects, reptiles and animals to its human beings. Wherever the invader tried to attack Africa he found it filled to the brim with a vivid, flame-flickering, dancing life of its own, ranging in size from the mosquito to the elephant. When three hundred years ago my ancestors landed at the southern extremity of Africa, there were not merely prancing bushmen and slant-eyed Hottentots to greet them but also hippopotamuses with the same portly shape and air as those Lord Mayors who carry the gold chains of office on their stomachs, kingly lions, royal leopards, rhinoceros as irritable as peppery generals whose livers have been ruined by whiskey and curry in the tropics, and wise old elephants, patient as elder statesmen, wading into the breakers to look the new arrivals over! I have often stayed in one of the oldest houses in Cape Town, which stands on the seashore and still bears the name "Leeuwenhof," the Court of Lions, so-called because when it was built the lions were prowling nightly in what has since become a lovely civilized garden.

Nor was this fullness, richness and variety of life confined merely to the animals. Inside the defences of this redoubtable African fortress of original life, man lived and developed an extraordinary varied and vivid being of his own. There was the pygmy bushman, the little yellow man with his Mongolian eye and enlarged posterior, who neither husbands animals nor cultivates the land but trusts himself to nature and the rhythm of the seasons like fish to the sea, and who feels far more secure in this natural environment than ever he does in the one that "superior" man presumed to give him. There was the Hottentot, taller and possessing a secret eye, who was more "advanced" in our understanding of the word in that he owned dogs and hump-backed cattle and walked slowly behind his fat nomadic herds, his skin shining like newly strung telephone wires in the sun. Then in the east there was the Bantu with his heavy slow-stepping grace, and in the west the Negro with his baroque sense of fate, and numbers of other sub-divisions and colourful Nilotic and Hamitic variants. Contrast those with Australia's one aboriginal race, and do you wonder that I call this development miraculous?

So for thousands and thousands of years this rich life was truly contained and nourished by Africa on African soil and uniquely in the African way. I know of no other life which has possessed for so long this seclusion and continuity, this privileged isolation from foreign influence and greed. It seems to me that Africa gives the most dramatic example of life developing from an invisible point in time where, as Euclid might have put it, history has as yet no size or magnitude but only position, right on into our own age, always following a development which was not according to man's idea of life so much as according to life's own plan for itself. For in this African development there was the minimum amount of conscious interference in life's processes; the minimum amount of direction from the producer in the desperate pantomime of our time.

In the last century, of course, the scene has changed brusquely. This picture which I have given you is vanishing fast, though it is still valid in large tracts of the great continent. The bushman is still living in the Kalahari Desert, just as he did in the

beginning of time. I have recently been there and I
have seen him in his natural and innocent society,
still using his love-making ritual, the cupid's bow,
which hitherto for me had been little more than an
image on a Greek vase. I have also been in sleeping-
sickness country just below the great escarpments
of Abyssinia and seen black people of superb physique, garlands of wild flowers round their necks,
marching towards me unexpectedly out of the sing-
ing grass and playing on pipes exactly like the Pipes
of Pan which, too, I had only known from Greek
vases. I assure you there is enough of this life still
left in Africa to show us what it was like before we
came on the scene. Indeed, it is odd when one con-
siders the efficiency with which we dig up old ruins
all over the world in order to get some idea of what
ancient man and his world was like, and then re-
members that here in Africa we have ancient man
still alive, his ancient spirit burning bright within
him, and yet we leave his mind despised, ignored
and utterly neglected. Allow me to give you one example of how automatic this under-valuation can
be. Some years ago when I was organizing an expedition to the great Kalahari Desert of Southern
Africa, two scientists of international repute arrived

with letters of introduction at my advanced base. They asked if they could accompany the expedition because they were doing research work on the bushman of Africa. When I asked what kind of research, they explained that they were making a comparative study of the head-measurements of primitive peoples all over the world. They described at length the methods they used and showed me an impressive catalogue of detail already observed. After a long while of this I asked, "What about the inside of their heads? Are you not interested in what goes on inside them?"

"That," they said with conclusive professional superiority, "is a different branch of science." Yet they were very upset because I saw no point in taking them with me. Over and over again I have been humbled by what goes on in the minds and hearts of these and other primitive peoples. When, as I have done, one takes part in this "life for life's sake," when one moves through its daily scene for a round of seasons, one no longer sees oneself as someone apart from nature and above and in command of life, but rather as someone small and helpless, yet immersed in a rich scheme of being for sheer being's sake. One realizes that it is not we who are filled with spirit or soul, but rather the dark and despised people about us. They have so much of it that it overflows into the trees, rocks, rivers, lakes, birds, snakes and animals that surround them. The bushman makes gods out of all the animals around him; the Hottentots kneel to an insect, the praying mantis; the Bantu listens to the spirits of his ancestors in the noise of his cattle stirring in their kraals of thorn at night, made restive by the roar of the lion and the hyena's werewolf wailing; the Negro appeases and invokes the gods in endless fetishes and images of wood and clay. But one and all they are humble parts of life and at one with it, knowing that, in order to get through their tiny, trembling day, they are in constant need of support from a power greater than themselves. They all have their own ways of evoking this support—elaborate rituals, strict codes of behaviour, colourful ceremonial evolved out of their experience of life—and their own social ethics in terms of which they are initiated into life and ushered out from it. They are poorer in almost every way than we and no more successful, perhaps, in these matters than we are. But in one great respect they are richer. Whatever happens to them, their lives are never lonely for lack of spirit nor do they find life wanting in meaning. To this day you have only to hear the bushman, Bantu, Hottentot or Negro laugh, to realize how true that still is.

Then suddenly we, European man, burst in upon this scene. As I have said, my own ancestors were among the first successfully to land at the southern cape of Africa three centuries ago, but the natural defences of greater Africa did not seriously begin to give way to outside invasion until about a hundred years ago, and only finally crumbled during the nineties of the last century. When that happened the white man could not have been less prepared for what he was about to find. A long period of pure reason, which had begun with the Reformation and been stimulated by the French Revolution, was deep at work in his spirit, setting him at variance with his intuitions and instincts. The materialism of the Industrial Revolution already dominated his values and motives; his mastery of the physical means of life and his increasing annihilation of distance together with the conquest of what he understood to be time, had already brought man far down the broad way to exceeding his humanity and setting himself up as a controller of destiny. Walking into Africa in that mood he was, by and large, quite incapable of understanding Africa, let alone of appreciating the raw material of mind and spirit with which this granary of fate, this ancient treasure house of the lost original way of life, was so richly filled. He had, it is true, an insatiable eye for the riches in the rocks, for diamonds and gold. But for the diamonds and gold of an ancient lost world sparkling in the many dark eyes raised in wonder and bewilderment to him, for the precious metal ringing true in the deep-toned laughter of the indigenous peoples round him, he had no interest. To this day if I want information about the stones and mineral deposits of Africa I am embarrassed by the richness of the material instantly placed at my disposal. Yet if I want information about the plants and grasses, as I recently did, I am staggered by the decline in the quality and quantity of the material offered to me. And when I want information that goes below the superficial mechanism of their society, about the peoples of Africa themselves, their spirits, languages and minds, about the things they find funny and the things they believe wonderful, I am dismayed and saddened by the terrible lack of material and interest generally displayed. I am certain all this is because European man arrived in

Africa already despising Africa and African beings. He arrived there, not for Africa's sake, but for what he could get out of Africa on his own behalf. He arrived as a superior person ready to impose himself and his way of living on Africa, not doubting for a second that his was the better way and that it was all for Africa's good. The same thing which made him despise the African made him despise the African's social organization, his goods and chattels, his agriculture, the way he tended his crops as well as his cattle. Chiefs, tribal organizations, witch doctors and ancient rituals were abolished swiftly by the administrator with his pen. And the settler and agricultural expert followed fast to impose their European cattle, their European seed and way of farming, upon Africa. The missionary, either in the van or close behind, came to abolish the black man's spirits, give him a new sense of sin, do away with his practice of religion as base superstition, and win him over to a new and superior white god. The rejection of Africa in all dimensions was as complete as it could possibly be. In the beginning there was some slight fighting resistance from the African, but looking back on it all now the wonder to me is that there was so little. I can only put it down to the fact that at first the African took the European at his own estimation of himself. The enormous power the European had over physical things, which you must remember were never merely physical things to the African but containers of all-powerful spirits, convinced him that the European was more than human.

I am old enough to remember the enormous hush that fell over Africa in the wake of the coming of European man. In the African heart there was a calm and tense air of expectation of growing wonders to come, and as a result there was also the most moving and wonderful readiness of the African to serve, to imitate and to follow the European, and finally an unqualified preparedness to love and be loved. My childhood memories of the light of that preparedness in African eyes and its absence in the same eyes today often keeps me awake at night. If you doubt me, remember the small forces that the white man had to use in his first barbarous conflicts. That was due not merely to the superiority of the white men's weapons in battle. Today we have even bigger and better weapons than we had then, yet the African has started to fight back against the white man in Kenya, for instance, as never before. No, I think the initial readiness of the black man to serve the white man was perhaps because, unconsciously, he had long waited for someone like the white man to come and bring him something which only the white man could provide. So, when he did come, it was as if it was in answer to some dream far back in the African mind and in response to some deep submerged hope that Africa had of the future. The white man's coming seemed to imply the fulfilment of a promise which had been made to the African far back by life in its first beginnings. If this were not so, I think the African would quickly have lost heart and died out of sheer discouragement as many an Indian tribe and nation died in the Americas, or as many Papuans and other South Sea islanders died at the coming of the white man in the Pacific. Yet the black man in Africa has not only multiplied but has gone on serving the white man in a way that is almost too good to be true. "Too good to be true." May I ask you to remember that phrase?

This period of the hush, of suspended indigenous development in Africa, was a moment of immense potentiality and hope in the contact between black and white. It contained great opportunity and possibilities for good, which the European at the time had not the power to understand. Often have I seen this period of innocence in the personal relationships between human beings. I have seen it once or twice, too, in the histories of people. I saw it in Indonesia after the last Japanese war. There was a moment then when the relief at the defeat of Japan left the whole of occupied Indonesia in a mood out of which something true, good and lasting might have instantly sprung. I saw the moment vanish and a distorted and twisted element come out of it with a mind and a will and a direction of its own, a form of distorted actuality which now has to live out its alloted span and die before anything else can take its place. In Africa, too, I see this moment of innocence and opportunity rapidly vanishing. I think it began to disappear after the First World War. I noticed then that the spell we had over the black man was broken, and I was so perturbed with this first intimation that later I wrote a book about it.*

Still, at that time, the situation was not too bad. But when I came back from this last war, wherever I went I was horrified by the change. Events that were rarities in my childhood days were common-

* *In a Province* (Hogarth Press, 1935) which today seems to have an odd prophetic ring about it.

place: ritual murder, flesh eating, secret societies raised against authority, lightning eruptions of violence and murder, and often apparently inexplicable outbreaks in areas that had known no unrest for a long time. These things were everywhere on the increase as were also the other classic signs of great inner unrest: a gathering drift of displaced persons into towns, the growing numbers of frustrated unemployed and unemployable intellectuals at street corners, the increase of political agitation and social confusion, the apparently senseless smashing of shop windows and inexplicable riots in civilized streets.

Before the war with Germany I wrote, "The windows of the individual mind are shattered long before stones are thrown in the street and the police put to flight by the mob. There is a riot in the human heart and the forces of law and order in the spirit are first overthrown by a nightmare horde. Already deep down in the human soul the individual is melting into the crowd." * In Africa the same sort of development could mean only one thing for me. The black African's sense of security and of oneness with life, had been shaken in a most

* Written in 1935.

profound way, his access to life's inmost meaning rudely barred. The spell of the European over him was not only breaking but his confidence in the European way of life was so shaken that, in a desperate effort to avert the disaster and annihilation which now seemed to threaten him from within, he turned back to the angry power of his disregarded, discredited and neglected spirits. Only appeasement of these spirits, as he sees it, can prevent him from losing his hurt aboriginal soul forever. For no matter how vicious are the forms wherein it expresses itself, or how effective the economic and materialistic trappings wherein it disguises itself, the conflict in Africa is, at heart, a battle about being and non-being, about having a soul of one's own or not having a soul at all.

We have a striking illustration of what I mean in the Mau-Mau activities in Kenya, for what has happened to the Kikuyu in Kenya is what has happened to so many other races in Africa. The white man has first discredited the African way of living and dealing with the forces of nature about and within, and then obliged him increasingly to live in a way which rejects the institutions, customs, initiation rites and rituals by which, for centuries, he has struck a balance with those overwhelming aspects of nature which are incomprehensible to reason and quite beyond conscious control and rational articulation. I do not want to imply that it was necessarily bad that this African way of living was discarded. It was inevitable in the nature of things that sooner or later it would either have to die of itself or else be rejected by the Africans themselves before they could move on to something more complete. But what is deplorable is that having discredited this ancient way of living we have not put an honourable alternative in its place. No human being or society, however self-sufficient and rational it may appear, can live without institutions that deal with those aspects of life which cannot be explained rationally. No community can be left indefinitely outside in the night of the human spirit, in the beast-infested jungle which lies beyond the conscious fortifications which civilized culture raises for *us* in life. If a community cannot get within the protection of those fortifications by fair means, then it will do so by foul. If civilized reason and conscious strength will not aid it, then animal cunning and brute force will. Having then destroyed the cultural defences of the Kikuyu people, it was imperative that we should

give them the protection of our way of life and free
access to our own institutions. It was all the more
imperative in the case of the Kikuyu because they
are one of the most intelligent African peoples. But
having destroyed their natural defences, we then
denied them our own. Having taken away their way
of life, we then made it impossible for them to acquire any other. Having supplanted their law by
ours, we then gave them no right to live as our
law demanded but rather forced them to drift suspended in dark acceptance of a state of non-being.
That is something that no human race can do and
survive. What most terrifies the primitive man is
not physical danger but the fear that he may lose
his soul. This is implicit in all his ritual, religion
and daily behaviour. I believe Mau-Mau is a desperate attempt on the part of the Kikuyu to prevent
such a loss of national soul. What is going on out
there at the moment is, in a deep primitive sense,
a war of religion. It may be a struggle for a form of
religion so crude and base that it must revolt all
civilized senses and one which the European is
forced to reject with all his power. But it is a war of
religion for all that. It is a fight of the Kikuyu for
their old Kikuyu gods. It is a battle, as the Romans

would have said, for the "ashes of their fathers and the temples of their gods."

I could give you many illustrations of similar processes and point out to you that, as a consequence of unenlightened white policy, somewhere in Africa's hidden being is piling up a sinister power of accumulated energy sufficient to shatter the world that is taking away its soul. Africa is being charged like one of the electronic piles used to split the atom. For Africa, from earth and beast up to the most intelligent of its indigenous children, is not letting this loss of soul take place without a terrible struggle. Even the soil of Africa, this ancient red soil founded on the original rock of the earth, is rebelling against European methods of agriculture and is carrying on a kind of continual "Mau-Mau" against the white man's crops and cattle in Africa. The soil will cooperate no longer and is either blown away in clouds of dust under the burning sun, or, during the rains, fills the rivers till they run red as blood to the sea or else bubble like porridge in the steaming marshes. The desert, too, is advancing on Cape Town at the rate of almost a mile a year, and the white man's expensive and rare European cattle grow sterile and feeble and are reduced to half their former size within a few short cattle generations in tropical Africa. The law of diminishing returns in imported European animal husbandry and agriculture in Africa has already set in. Those wise Europeans who have studied Africa most closely have read a warning lesson in what has happened to the cattle and goods they brought with them from Europe and today are turning to the despised African's humped beasts in order to rejuvenate their own European animals and redress the mounting negative balances in their banks. Some of the wisest of them have even rejected their European stock and bred this despised indigenous material with the same care and skill that their forefathers used on the indigenous breeds of Europe, and as a result have been so rewarded by the response of Africa that they have grown rich in the process. But elsewhere the revolt is all of a piece; the reaction of indigenous soil and indigenous man to the white man's attempt to deny Africa and her children their own unique being is one and complete.

The only thing that is surprising is not the revolt but the white man's astonishment that it should have happened. When this hush of which I have spoken first fell on Africa, when all these multitudi-

nous African races that had been either plundering
and raiding and fighting with one another for
thousands of years, or else leading peaceful lives
at one with nature, resolving their own dark energies in elaborate and meaningful ritual, when all
this suddenly ceased and the black man everywhere put on a dutiful face and meekly did whatever he was told, no matter how contradictory to his
past behaviour; when all this dutiful goodness suddenly appeared on the face of this ancient land you
might have thought that someone among the white
people would have asked, But where has all this
terrific psychic energy that expressed itself in war,
migration, nomadic circulation and elaborate ritual
gone? What has become of it? What is it doing? How
is it expressing itself? For surely it is an ineluctable
law of physics that energy can be transmuted but
never annihilated. You might have imagined that
the white man would have realized that he had to
do something about directing the black man's energy
into legitimate channels, that he had to give him a
form of living, equip him liberally with all the safety
devices and compensations with which our culture
has provided us. Unfortunately no one in Africa
asked these questions. Instead, the sudden sub-

servience of the African was taken only as proof absolute of the overwhelming "superiority" of the white man. The "inferiority" of the African was exploited to the full in exactly the same way as, during the past one hundred and fifty years, our modern industrial age has exploited less conscious states of mind of the socially backward classes of civilized communities. So when I said just now that the sudden subservience of the African had been "too good to be true" and asked you to remember that expression, it was because of this. And this brings me to the main title of my talk.

My title "Mata Kelap" is actually a Malay phrase. "Mata" is the Malay for eye, and "Kelap" for dark. It means the dark eye. It is an expression which is used in Sumatra and Java to describe a curious and disturbing social phenomenon. Socially speaking, the Malays, Sumatrans and Javanese are the best behaved people I have ever encountered. On the surface they are an extremely gentle, refined, submissive people. In fact, the word "Malay" comes from "malu" which means "gentle," and gentleness is a quality prized above all others among the Malays and their neighbours. In their family life, in their submission to traditional and parental authority, they are among the most obedient people on earth, and in doing what they take to be their communal duties they are models that would rejoice the most Prussian of hearts. But every now and then something very disturbing happens. A man who has behaved in this obliging manner all his life and who has always done his duty by the outside world to perfection, suddenly finds it impossible to continue doing so. Overnight he revolts against goodness and dutifulness and, knife in hand, goes out and murders everyone who imposed such goodness upon him, father, mother, wife, children, head of the village, or the planter to whom he has been such an exemplary steward. Now, when that happens to a man they say in those gentle emerald islands that he has gone "Mata Kelap"; that his eye has darkened within him.* In those same islands I was to see "Mata Kelap" on a national and not merely an individual scale, just as we have all seen a similar inky blackness slowly gather in the eyes of some of the most respected European nations, such as the blue German eye. I could enlarge on this European parallel, but I have time only to say that what is

* It is significant, too, that the ghost which troubles Malayan imagination most is a spirit who smashes things.

happening on a national level in Africa today is the first appearance of "Mata Kelap" on the African continent. Mau-Mau is the most dramatic manifestation we have had yet that the African eye is losing its light and darkening everywhere around us.

Again one asks, if this is so, why is the European behaving as he is? Why cannot he see what he is doing to Africa and correct his ways in time? But all these questions bring me to what I consider to be the most sinister element of all. I myself believe that the European's own eye is so darkened that he can no longer see himself or the things round about him in their full reality. The inner light, "the natural fire within the dark wood of life," as Dante put it, by which man once lived, is being put out and darkness is welling up like a sea both within and without him. I think the European is blindly and ignorantly provoking all these events in Africa because, in his deepest nature, he is provoking them in himself.

Ever since the Reformation, European man has been increasingly at war with himself, and certain aspects of his nature which he has found particularly useful and rewarding for producing his own type of civilization and culture have been developed excessively at the expense of others, thus doing violence to a very deep and real part of himself. This is not necessarily a bad thing. Up to a point it is the way in which all civilizations have come about. It is, if you like, the Promethean sin which all communities commit in order to enable their culture to evolve. But even such a noble sin, if it is not to lead to disaster, must keep within its own classic proportions. Even virtue owes homage to proportion. If it cannot learn the discipline of proportion freely from within, it has to learn it from disaster without, for whatever goes too far begets a violent reaction in order that it may be brought back into position. Unfortunately it appears to be the rule of life that societies find it almost impossible, without disaster in the physical world, to reverse an outworn evolutionary process. Except for that wonderful creative moment in our history when the two extremities of human nature—the natural, instinctive pagan element and the rational, conscious, forward-moving Christian awareness—came close enough to produce that flash of lightning which still dazzles our imagination and which we call the Renaissance, except for that moment of rebirth and awakening of modern man, we have swung to an extreme wherein the natural man within us not only has had very little honour but also his rich intuitive and instinctive promptings have been thrown summarily out of the courts of our reason, just as the aborigines of our time have been despised and rejected by Western man.

In a profound sense every man has two halves to his being: he is not one person so much as two persons trying to act in unison. I believe that in the heart of each human being there is something which I can only describe as a "child of darkness" who is equal and complementary to the more obvious "child of light." Whether we know it or not we all have within us a natural instinctive man, a dark brother, to whom we are irrevocably joined as to our own shadow. However much our conscious reason may reject him, he is there for good or ill, clamouring for recognition and awareness and a fair share of life just as the less conscious black man of Africa is struggling and clamouring for life, light and honour in our societies. I need not emphasize how the rational, calculating, acutely reasoning and determined human being that Western man has made of himself has increasingly considered this side of himself not as a brother but as an enemy, capable, with his upsurges of rich emotion and colourful impulses, of wrecking conscious man's carefully planned and closely reasoned way of existence.

I find some confirmation of this in the violence of our present-day colour prejudice. Hitherto this violence had not existed in Europe. When my forefathers landed more than three hundred years ago in the Cape of Good Hope, the colour prejudice was much less marked, and today we have the million "coloured" people of the Cape colony as proof of it. In the traditional ritual of the Christian churches, too, one of the three wise men of the East was a black man and his presence among the three sages who attended Christ in his crib at Bethlehem seemed necessary to make the symbolism of the event complete in European imagination. But in recent generations this colour prejudice among Europeans has become so powerful and destructive that it threatens to break out in increasing bloodshed in Africa. Significantly, too, everywhere in the world it has become more powerful and explosive according to the extent to which the distance has widened between overrational, specialized modern man and his natural roots. This separation of the white man with his bright morning face from his own dark rejected brother within, increases with frightening acceleration. So prejudice against the black skin of the natural African has deepened and made it a dangerous symbol, for now the white man in Africa sees reflected in the natural dark man round him that dark aspect of himself which he has rejected. Consequently he confuses the reflection without with the dark reality within, and without hesitation engages in fruitless and mutually disastrous battle with it.

We have talked all through this century of the white man's burden in Africa, yet what fatal irony there is in the phrase. Would it not be more accurate at the moment to talk of the black man's burden? I refer of course to this burden of terrible unconscious projection which modern European man thrusts upon the natural African who, by reason of his primitive instinctual life and "participation almost mystical" in his natural environment, is such a suitable container for it. Yet it is this very projection, outcome of the insidious civil war raging in the innermost being of modern man, which prevents the white man from ever seeing the black man as he really is. The white man can see in the black man only those aspects which confirm and justify his own projection and enable it to pass itself off as an outward and genuinely objective condition—which it is not. The results for both parties, of course, are deplorable. Since the European possesses physical power, this dreadful confusion compels him to create a form of society wherein the black man is condemned to play only that part which the increasingly exacting projection of the white man demands of him. The black man is thereby prevented from being himself and from living out his own unique being. He is like Adam in the Garden after he had tasted the forbidden fruit of the tree of knowledge, standing among the leaves still trembling with the magnetic nearness of the Old Testament God of Judgment and Justice. A power greater than himself banishes the African from the garden of his archaic state forever. The white man and his determined, unrecognizable projection stand in the way, refusing him the forward thrust of life, denying him the right to be his changing self. Behind him an archangel with a flaming sword seals the ancient gate forever; before him a thin-lipped white sentry with a machine-gun bars the way. The black man, too, therefore, has an unlived aspect of himself, a darker brother within, which constant denial daily makes great with the spirit of revenge and powerful with unused energies, and which is fast growing into an angry giant about to burst his bonds and use his strength like a colossus.

Meanwhile, the same processes have gone on developing in the white man. His unlived aspect, too, the despised and rejected dark brother of his own being, has grown greater and daily more terrible. Up to now these things in life have ended only in one way. The unlived aspects in the two opposites overwhelm their oppressors, the conscious restraints that have imprisoned them for so long break loose and they interlock in fatal battle. After the catastrophic demonstrations that this century has given us of the lengths to which the European social animal will go in projecting into the world round him this quarrel within himself, we have no longer any excuse for not recognizing this technique in the lives of nations. Let us revert again to terms of energy, for thereby we can use an impersonal idiom native to the problem. In physics one cannot introduce a negative charge of electricity in a given field without instantly inducing an equal and opposite charge of positive electricity. No matter how great may be your one-sided charge, an equal and opposite keeps pace and parallel with it until finally

both become so powerful that they leap the space
which separates one from the other and make the
zig-zag spark we call electricity. A negative individual and racial projection behaves in exactly the
same way. We can give it any name we please according to the level of life on which our energies are
engaged. If we are Socialists we can see it as a class
war; if Marxists, as a struggle between capital and
labour; if vitalists and mechanists, as a battle between idealism and materialism; if philosophers and
artists we see it as the unresolved battle between the
Apollonian and Dionysian, or the classic and romantic urges; if priests, as Christianity versus pa-
ganism; and if we are a South African statesman we
see it as the struggle of black versus white. But
basically I believe it is this hypothesis of the unlived
aspect of self in man and his communities resorting
to expression by foul means because it has been denied the fair means, which explains the confusion
and explosive prejudices of our time. Above all, only
this explains life's strange need of the terrible arbi-
tration of war and disaster in living creative issues.
The rational, cultured, scientific, progressive Germany of 1914 gives admirable illustration of this.
As Germany grew steadily from an obscure elec-

torate of the Holy Roman Empire and expanded into the great German Reich, as she grew more successful and powerful in the demonstrable world without, so she became charged with a sinister negative energy within. This sinister fever mounted in the German spirit in proportion to her success in the material world throughout the whole nineteenth century. As tension between darkness and light in the German soul mounted it was violently projected onto Germany's neighbours, quickly inducing among them an opposite concentration which expressed itself politically in a rapidly expanding system of defensive alliances. When this moment arrives in the spirit of either an individual or a nation, the fruits of that spirit, its vision and its thinking, cease to be contemporary. The human spirit then falls back on one discarded and discredited bastion after the other until, in the end, a hungry mythology takes over and, alas, the mythology which took over in the German heart and mind was a particularly frightening one. So far as I know, German mythology is the only mythology in which the forces of evil are finally triumphant. For in *Götterdämmerung* the cosmic scene closes, you may remember, with the forces of darkness streaming over the rainbow bridge to defeat the gods of light and their companionate order. Could there be a more accurate description of what has happened twice to the German spirit in this century?

In Africa the process has not yet reached that point, but the spirit of the white man has built up a terrible negative charge. The white man's "no" to the black man is daily more uncompromising and automatically induces an equal and opposite charge in the spirit of the black man. On both sides the eye has darkened and still is darkening. Anatole France said that human beings frequently kill one another over the words they use, whereas if only they had understood the meaning the words were trying to convey they would have embraced. There is a higher level to that truth. I wonder if you remember the legend of the white and the black knight in the saga of the Round Table? Two knights, one in black armour and one in white, were riding through a dark and dangerous wood in search of a chivalrous errand when they met. Visors down because of probable danger they challenged one another and, without further explanation, fought. They fought until they were both wounded to death and finally lay stretched out on the grass beside each other. Then, in dying, they uncovered their heads—and saw that they were brothers.

Perhaps this implication that the black man and the white man could be brothers sounds too fanciful in view of what is happening in Africa today. Yet there are the proverbs of many nations which suggest that hatred is akin to love. I suggest to you, therefore, that the struggle in Africa is so deadly and tragic just because, secretly, the black natural man in Africa attracts the European no matter how much he consciously rejects him. I say this with confidence because, after all, I was born in Africa and have not only lived with the prejudices of which I am speaking but have also shared them. Then one day I realized that far back in my childhood there was a moment when none of these prejudices had existed in me. I discovered in looking back that the real kings, queens and princes, the witches and the wizards and magicians and all the vivid fairy-tale personalities who gave my childhood a richer meaning were not the virtuous, disapproving Europeans but our black, yellow and copper-coloured servants, almost all of whom have long since vanished, though their names still make music in me. It was they who played a part in my imagination which no European could ever usurp. I suspect that at a deep level the same thing is true of my countrymen in South Africa. And, I suspect that if the European in Africa could only rediscover and honour in his imagination this natural moment at the beginning of his own life, then this unnatural tension would begin to disappear. At the present, of course, there is no outward sign that this will happen.

Anyway, it is not part of my talk tonight to tell you how I think such a rediscovery of this, our lost and legitimate natural self, can come about. My main object has been merely to describe to you what I consider to be the inner origins of this unrest in Africa. But may I add this. I seem to remember that Dr. Jung says somewhere that the aspect of themselves which human beings sacrifice in the attainment of a given object in their lives is reborn *alive* and comes back after many years, knife in hand, demanding to sacrifice that which sacrificed it. I think in this we have a picture of the dilemma, not only of Africa, but of the whole modern world. The whole problem of modern culture expresses the need for some transcendent factor or purpose wherein neither white nor black, neither natural nor thinking man, will have to be sacrificed to one another but both joined and made complete in one transcending purpose. After all, the two opposites of electricity need no longer be expressed through the bright and dangerous medium of lightning but can now be transformed and resolved together into a source of creative energy.

At the beginning of this talk I suggested that there were at least four dimensions in which this African unrest had to be considered. All that remains for me is to give you what I believe is the master container of all those four dimensions. I now want to suggest to you that this four-dimensional conflict which rages in Africa is contained in each individual human being. I want to suggest that the unrest in Africa, in all its facets, European, cosmic, global and African, is plainly an *extension* of our own individual unrest. This may seem to you absurd. How can that which is cosmic and universal be reduced to something so small? But it is, for me, no idle coincidence that the most significant discovery in the physical world of this age has been the fact that the greatest and most unimaginable power resides in the smallest possible organization of matter. The force which threatens to blow the world asunder resides not in the clouds or mountains but in the invisible heart of the atom. The inner force, too, which, like the power of the atom, can either remake or shatter civilization resides in the smallest unit of society, the individual. The individual is the secret advance base from which this power sets out to invade committee rooms, mothers' meetings, county councils, parliaments, continents and nations. I think that is why Africa is so meaningful for us all today.

I travel about the world a great deal and everywhere I am impressed by the interest taken in the conflict in Africa. In countries that have no cultural or historical associations with Africa I find this intense, extraordinary interest in what is happening there. Even I who was born in Africa have experienced again and again a need which made no rational sense to me to return and explore Africa. Then one night, sitting alone in the bush in Africa with nothing but my black bearers around me, suddenly I realized the meaning of my own compulsion, and perhaps, too, the explanation of the world's extraordinary interest in Africa. I realized in a flash that I walked Africa in this manner because only thus was I able to walk among the mysteries and uncomprehended complexities of my own heart and mind. I discovered that I travelled in Africa in this way because it brought me to unknown places in my own uncomprehended spirit which I could not have reached in any other manner. Perhaps therein reside the miracle and the meaning of Africa for all of us. Modern man with his grievous and crippling realization of having lost the sense of his own beginnings, with his agonizing feeling of great and growing estrangement from nature, finds that life holds up Africa like a magic mirror miraculously preserved before his darkening eyes. In this great glass of time the inmost reflection of his ancient, timeless spirit stares out at him, and he can, could he but realize it, rediscover there his despised and rejected natural self, recognizing before it is too late the full horror of his stubborn rejection of it.

There is a memory that has lived with me all my life from childhood in Africa which gives living illustration of this point. As children we used to take our mirrors, stand them on the ground in front of our tame baboons and then watch the creatures as for the first time they saw their own faces reflected back at them. It was amusing because the baboons could not realize that what they were looking at in the mirror was the reflection of themselves. The mechanism of reflection was quite beyond their comprehension and they could not accept the ugly, grimacing, increasingly irritable features staring back at them as their own. The only explanation of what they saw in the mirror was that there was another baboon in front of them, so they promptly looked for the stranger beast. They tried to touch its face, but felt only the glass against their purple fingers. They looked again and again behind the mirror, but the elusive creature could not be found. The only solution in the end was to pick up the mirror and smash it to pieces on the ground in their rage!

This I believe is a profound image of what happens in life and in Africa today. People and countries are mirrors to one another. They are, of course, also themselves just as the mirror is itself and not what it reflects, but they rarely recognize themselves; mostly they see what is hidden within themselves reflected in one another. The capacity to differentiate reflector and reflection in the many-dimensional realm of the living spirit and being of man is still primitive and relatively undeveloped in all of us, and future ages, no doubt, will laugh at us for this as we laughed at the baboon. I believe the greatest of all the mirrors of our age is Africa. We all, East and West and bewildered twentieth-century man, stare into it as if hypnotized, but, like the baboons, we do not see and recognize in it the reflection of our own hidden selves. Nevertheless, the interest of the world is compelled by events in Africa because, unconsciously, the world apprehends that Africa may hold the secret of its own lost and hidden being. Without this miraculously preserved Africa, without this land and its unbroken allegiance to the original charter and meaning of life, this timely reflection might not be possible. Let us pray therefore that we all realize that it is also ourselves we are looking at in Africa and not destroy this precious magic mirror in our rage—as so many vanished civilizations before us have destroyed theirs to their own undoing.

The Discussion

"O frati," dissi, *"che per cento milia*
perigli siete giunti all' occidente,
a questa tanto picciola vigilia

de' vostri sensi, ch' e del rimanente,
non vogliate negar l'esperienza,
di retro al sol, del mondo senza gente.

Considerate la vostra semenza:
fatti non foste a viver come bruti,
ma per seguir virtute e conoscenza." *

Flame of Ulysses to Dante in Hell.

---

* "Brothers," I said, "who now have reached the West
By conquering a hundred thousand dangers,
Deny not to that little span of life—
The brief allotment of your waking hours
That yet remains to you—experience
Of that unpeopled world behind the sunset.
Consider from what noble seed you spring:
You were created not to live like beasts,
But for pursuit of virtue and of knowledge!"

Translated from *The Divine Comedy* of Dante Alighieri by Lawrence Grant White. New York: Pantheon Books, 1948.

QUESTION

Mr. Chairman, I have followed what Colonel van
der Post has said with great interest, but I must confess there is something which is far from clear to
me. I refer to that part of his talk where he says that
the unrest in Africa is in the first place unrest in
time. I am not at all certain as to what he means by
that. The concept of time as another dimension is,
of course, not unfamiliar to us. Many of us who are
not physicists or mathematicians can conceive of it
as that, but then mainly as an impersonal dimension.
But he talked of it tonight as something which possessed a nature of its own. I wonder if he could say
more about it; otherwise it is difficult to understand
what practical contribution this rather vague concept can make to the understanding of so absorbing
and urgent a problem as he has outlined.

ANSWER

I would like to be more explicit but I cannot
really carry my meaning much further. It may be

that somewhere in some Olympian abstraction of life, time is a completely empty dimension. But I was thinking of it as time revealed in this universe of ours, as time made meaningful in life. In that sense I could tell you only what it meant to me in the hope that thereby I could convey an aspect of meaning to you. But this idea of time being something more than a "when" is not original or new. We in the West with our sustained concentration on the visible and external world have been obsessed with the working of time without and about us and have regarded it almost entirely as a *measure*. Other ages and other civilizations have had a different approach. For instance, I am now reading a Chinese book which is one of the oldest books in the world; the characters used to express its meaning are the oldest known in China and they emerge warm and alive straight from the mind of legendary men. It is clear to me from this book that time in the most creative periods of Chinese history was never considered to be an empty, unilateral thing. The Chinese regarded it as a vital element of life like the invisible air which surrounds us but without which we cannot live. They observed its effects not merely in the world without but also deep within their own

natures. As a result they believed that it added
something uniquely its own to every given moment
and that many of man's misfortunes were due to
his ignorance of the fundamental laws of this element. They believed that all life at the same moment
unknowingly shared the same time characteristics
and according to differing living capacities was affected thereby. So they became interested not in the
sequence of events but rather in the rounding qualities and coincidences of actuality. Coincidences and
chance were never idle to them but rather manifes-
tations of some law of time of whose workings they
were inadequately aware. In fact, these ancient Chinese scientists were so sure of their touch in this
inner dimension that they fashioned a means, based
on observation of the workings of chance and cir-
cumstance in the lives of individuals over thousands
of years, for determining the inter-relationship between a given moment in individual life and the
greater moment of time enclosing it, a process which,
before I had discovered this meaningful Chinese
concept, I had written of as "the great together-
nesses of life." In terms of this concept I can only
draw your attention to what is universal in the character of African unrest and suggest, like the Chi-

nese oracle, that these coincidences of unrest are not idle, but on the contrary a fundamental element in the workings of the undiscovered laws of our time. To that extent the problem of which I have spoken is unrest of time.

That brings me to the second half of the question: what practical importance can "this rather vague concept" possess? I am not at all certain that this idea is so vague as is thought. Tested by reason and outward senses it may appear to be because these instruments were not designed for that purpose. But there are other equally valid functions in the totality of the human spirit which should help us to understand that this way of looking at African unrest is of immense inner significance and therefore of great practical consequence. For if this unrest is also of time then it relieves us, in part, of an impossible burden of responsibility. It means that this terrible problem is not entirely of our own making and that we are experiencing "The sorrows of our proud and angry dust" which the poet tells us "are from eternity and shall not fail." It means that there is an aspect of the problem which originates in time and which time alone can and shall resolve. It means we are not alone, and that if we look after the seconds, the years will take care of themselves. For time is not merely a "when" and a "what" but also a "how." Every farmer knows he can decide on the day and hour when he takes his bull to the cow, but between conception and the birth of the calf there is a "how" of time, a fixed proportion that has to be observed and honoured and which the farmer can do nothing about. Yet, simple as it is, frequently in human affairs this aspect of time is ignored. We are continually ruining good intentions and plans by refusing to reckon with the living, organic time element native to them. We try to force impossibly quick solutions, to decree today what can only be born tomorrow. The international scene is full of striking illustrations of failure brought about by denying time its legitimate role in counsels and decisions, trying to produce nice, right-minded little calves in ten weeks instead of ten months and merely provoking endless abortions in the process. I will give you an example of what I mean in Africa. My countrymen in South Africa at this moment are trying consciously to determine what shall be the shape of their society in the centuries to come. They are trying to legislate what role the black man shall play in their society so that an "uncontaminated" white society shall continue in existence for the next thousand years or more. They are taking on themselves an improper and impossible role that belongs only to time. If they left it also to time, I am certain that long before a thousand years the causes that today make black skins so repugnant to them will have vanished. But they do not understand or trust time, and in going against it they are, I am certain, precipitating the disaster they want to avoid.

There is yet another sense wherein time is of even greater practical importance, for time is uniquely the way of the spirit. It is the long road upon which the sun not only rises in the morning but upon which the glow of a star shattered a million light years ago overtakes the tired and far-travelled soul in the dead hour of the night. It is the desert track where intimation of the meaning-to-be catches up with the harassed caravan of humanity and comes, like a stranger, to warm its hands by a flickering fire. It is the great plain wherein what is unconscious in the spirit journeys into consciousness. Above all it is the rhythm without which there is no music in the heart; it is the will of the spirit to live and to be whole. And this is not mysticism. It is the kind of language one is forced to use when one's awareness brushes against an abiding mystery of life. It is just plain *mysterious*—for at heart life is utterly mysterious and in consequence is a matter also for natural faith and trust. Without this essential acceptance of mystery our consciousness is deprived of a vital proportion of reality and tends to be excessive and arrogant in its claims. We need a sense of wonder, for it is part of our wholeness and keeps us humble and our minds in position. One of the more harmful by-products of the excessively one-sided and scientific concentration of the past centuries has been the tendency to eliminate in men the sense of the mystery of life and to depreciate any feelings which lie outside the range of our conscious awareness. The process, too, was made easier as Western civilization became more and more a metropolitan culture and man's conquests in the physical world increased the distance between him and nature. So his natural contacts with the great mysteries steadily became more remote. I shall never forget the first night of this last war. I was walking down Regent Street in London in our first black-out. Suddenly everywhere round me I heard people exclaiming, "Look at the stars, aren't they wonderful!" and I realized then that there were thousands of people round me who had never before seen the night walking naked and unashamed into the quiet and fullness of time.

Africans so far have not lost that contact with mystery, and its influence on their make-up is immense. You cannot understand them and the violence that is being done to their spirit unless you first understand that. Fortunately science today is moving out of that shallow nineteenth century depression and more and more acknowledges and respects the unknown. In the past the astronomer faced mystery without. But now already in physics the scientist has found that matter which feels so solid beneath his feet becomes, on investigation, more and more insubstantial, eccentric, mysterious and "unlawful" until finally at the far end of his electronic microscope it melts into thin air like Prospero's vision, leaving him with "such stuff as dreams are made on." Indeed, the correspondence between this "astronomy of the atom" and the astronomy of our stars is a matter for wonder. So I can only repeat that restoring the sense of mystery to our spirit, letting it once more into our brittle calculations, allowing it to lend dignity and meaning to human suffering and perplexity is a wholesome and healing thing. In this connection I always think of that wonderful moment of resolution in the tragedy of King Lear. When Lear's cause is finally lost and he and the daughter are sent to prison and death, one might imagine that his unhappiness could not be greater, but, on the contrary, he turns to Cordelia and says—and this is the wonder of it—that they shall sing like birds in a cage and take upon themselves "the mystery of things" as if they "were God's spies." And that, could we but see it, is what we are—God's spies going ahead of the meaning-to-come in a great wilderness wherein there is as yet no meaning, and in the heroic process taking upon ourselves the mystery of all things. That sense of mystery is the great seal of our authority, and the practical difference it makes to our being and becoming is immense. That sense of mystery works in and through us in time.

QUESTION

I am the widow of a missionary who dedicated his
life to work among the black people in Africa. I
regret that I have a strong impression that you do
less than justice to what missionaries have done for
Africa. You imply that all they have done is to take
away and give nothing in return. You speak of
Mau-Mau, for instance, as a battle of the Kikuyu
for their gods, as a battle to retain some gods rather
than have no gods at all. You say we took away
their religion and gave them no honourable alternative in its place. Surely, that is a terrible distortion
of the facts. We offered them our God instead of
theirs. Is not that an honourable alternative? We
gave them Christianity instead of heathenism. I
am told that one of the most remarkable things that
is happening in Kenya is the heroic fight the ill-
armed and dangerously exposed Kikuyu converts to
Christianity are waging against Mau-Mau. The
truth surely is that the Kikuyu were not faced with a
choice between "no God and their gods" but be-

tween our faith and theirs. Most of them chose to return to the basest of their own beliefs, hence the conflict with Mau-Mau and the challenge of ritual
murder that faced us in places like Basutoland
where we ourselves worked.

ANSWER

I am very glad you have asked me these questions.
I debated with myself for a long time before deciding to bring Mau-Mau into this talk. I knew it was
a dangerous and potentially misleading illustration,
for there is so much emotion about in regard to that
tragic event that my chances of being misunderstood
were numerous. Yet I decided I could not shirk the
issue, for here, too, the "great imponderables," as I
call them elsewhere, seem to have been left out of
the general reckoning. It is so easy to see the bestial,
barbaric elements in which this phenomenon reveals itself, but what of the hidden, frustrated and
naturally aspiring sources from whence they sprang?

So first let us be agreed about the level on which
we are discussing this problem. It is a level on which
we are trying to consider things for what they are
within themselves before going over to the emotions

they provoke in us, a level above blame and where all our efforts are concentrated on understanding the specific nature and gravity of the phenomenon which confronts us. On this level I assure you I had no intention or desire to imply the least criticism of what missionaries have done in Africa. The situation is enough in itself without burdening it with retrospective blame. One of the most common errors in contemporary judgments is our knack of wrenching people and events out of their proper time context and assessing them as if they were part of the contemporary sequence of things. We are now at a summit of painful experience and fateful disaster. We are like dwarfs perched on the shoulders of a giant, and it is easy enough for us to see further than the giant and criticize the past. I may not myself, at this time, believe in specialized missions bent on converting people from one faith to another. If I believe in missions at all it is in the unsoliciting mission of *example*. But only the most wilful of prejudices could blind us to the great and lasting good that missionary effort once brought to Africa, and had I been born in the early nineteenth century even I might have been as ardent a supporter of the great missionary movement in England as the great Dr.

Philip himself, who gave his name to the village in which I was born.

Yet in this matter of the great missionary effort in Africa we are once more up against our basic image of the mirror and the reflection in the mirror. The New Testament, which is so charged with inner truth, has its own poignant evidence of our inner capacity to confuse the mirror with what it reflects. Christ warned his disciples against the danger of this confusion when he spoke of the mote in the neighbour's eye and the beam in our own. One can hardly carry this implication too far. In fact, I would suggest that often the mote in our neighbour's eye is merely a reflection of the beam in our own, and that perhaps were it not for this reflection in the eye of our neighbour we would not be aware of our own beam. There is a moment, therefore, when confusion of the two is innocent and quite inevitable. That is how life works, how it draws us on. Life holds up the physical visible world as a mirror before us so that we can be provoked into learning how to recognize our own reflection and so detach it from the rest, accepting the consequences in the process. The confusion only becomes culpable if we persist in it after experience and repeated disaster have clearly discredited our previous path. But that said, let us go further and look at the problem not in relation to any specialized aspect but in relation to the contemporary whole wherein both it and the missionary are contained.

Now in that whole, I repeat, the choice to the primitive African presents itself as a choice between his ancient beliefs or no beliefs at all. We may offer the African our faith every Sunday as we offer it to our diminishing selves, but at heart he is not impressed by that. He is like a child who is influenced not by what his parents profess but rather by what they do. The African today is growing less and less impressed by what we preach in Church and profess in parliament. He is influenced by what we do. He goes by the example we set. He may pick up a certain Christian patter and find it convenient for the practical business of living to wear a Christian mask, as we do. But it does not take him long to see that there is a dark gulf between what we profess in Church on Sundays and practise in the week. With such example all about him is it surprising that he does likewise? Do not think that I am not aware of a great number of good and heroic exceptions. You have mentioned the Kikuyu Christians and I can add greatly to your list. I would only say this: examine the exceptions and you will find that in general they have come about in response to the force of example set them by individual missionaries and priests of exceptional character who have practised what they preached. The response in the main has been to the man rather than to the church. One of the most winning qualities of my black countrymen is that they have an instinct for faith and a preparedness to follow and be truly led. That is why it is so terrible that what we offer, by and large, is a limited-liability Christianity which is little more than a modern social convenience and more convenient to the white men than the black. We, alas, know less and less the meaning of the master passion of the spirit which once drove through Christian man. With us spirit is fast declining into mere intellect, an agile and adroit monkey that obliges us with good reasons for doing bad things. If this sounds harsh look at what is happening in my own country. Some churches, it is true, still try to preach and lecture the European in Africa into a more Christian state of mind. But already the biggest Christian church there has ranged itself solidly behind the legislation which seeks to perpetuate the sharp-edged colour prejudices of my countrymen. This church has even admitted colour prejudice in its own observances and decreed that white and black shall not worship in the same buildings. Learned theologians of this church quote the Bible to justify this large-scale denial to the African of his rights and opportunities as a man, and his dignity which is equal to any before God. Do you call this Christianity holding out an honourable alternative to the African? Do you wonder that the African finds it impossible to have much hope and respect for that sort of faith? For the African in his archaic way can experience the blast of the ancient spirit of man to the full. He is so filled with it that it overflows from him even into the inanimate objects round him. He is so dominated by it that he is incapable of giving the physical world its own validity—and pays heavily for his failure. He never dreams of denying his instinctual soul and there are plenty of illustrations of this in African history. There is, for instance, the national near-suicide of the Amaxosa in the last century. I told you the story in detail two years ago, but for those who did not hear me then, briefly it is this. On the word of one person, a mere girl who, like Joan of Arc, heard voices and dreamed a strange persistent dream and whom their witch-doctor prophet in his archaic concept declared truly inspired, the Amaxosa killed all their cattle, goats, sheep, hens and chickens. And this merely on a dream promise that once all the living things that the Amaxosa owned had been destroyed, all their dead ancestors would return to life and help them to drive the white man back into the sea. They carried out to the final disastrous letter this injunction from the unseen world of the spirits in whom they trusted. No Christian crusader on the way to the Holy City ever observed a sacred vow more faithfully than they did. Of course on the appointed day not a single ancestor or slaughtered bullock rose from the dead and the great Amaxosa nation nearly perished in the famine that followed. The story to this day is quoted as an example of what a gullible, superstitious and backward lot Africans are. To me it has always been a most moving and humbling illustration of how great is the African's capacity and need for a lived and living faith. Do you think that, in dealing with such people, a cerebral Christianity, an argumentative religion, a faith *en tête* as the French would put it, which is increasingly incapable of transforming thinking and moral precept into living emotion can be an alternative? You mentioned ritual murder in Basutoland. I described a ritual murder in very great detail to you all before in this very place, and I told you how several of the people who took part in the murder belonged to the mission church. I told you how they kept their black victim for months in the bed of a river within sight of the cross of the church on the hill above it without seeing anything incongruous in their behaviour. But don't we, too, keep our own religion in a special Sunday compartment all its own? I wish I had time to run through the detail of this particular murder with you again, but I can only remind you that we agreed last time that it was, in the archaic sense, a responsible social act performed by responsible people with the utmost seriousness, in the belief that thereby they would benefit the community and relieve it of an intolerable anxiety. The church on the hill had failed to do this, so they turned back to the ritual which, rightly or wrongly, they believed had brought them safely through danger in the past. I myself find it impossible to judge these things to be merely murder. In society punishment can, so often, be just a lazy way out of a difficult situation, and at best it is only a half-measure, and society should realize the extent to which it has been accessory to the criminal fact. I do not know how we can be morally justified in hanging and punishing people in Africa for this sort of thing so long as we do so little to change the conditions and circumstances, largely of our creation, that drive them to it. Unfortunately the tendency in all systems is to think that once a crime has been punished society has done its bit. For my part, I can only repeat that to offer the African our faith *without the accompaniment of the way of life and opportunity which that faith demands* is to offer him no faith at all.

I see Mau-Mau and the ritual murder you mentioned in these ways. I see them as signs of how deeply our failure to integrate the displaced African into our own way of life has penetrated. I see them as a sign of our failure to give Africans a sense of community, purpose and being with us, and evidence of the intolerable anxieties induced in them by our failure. I see our failure as a reflection of European man's own disintegration and a desperate call for a supreme act of renewal and reintegration on his part.

QUESTION

Assuming that we have not held out an honourable alternative to the African, and that his own way is Mau-Mau, is not Mau-Mau therefore right? I had a feeling as I listened to your answer to the last question that we could not blame the African for Mau-Mau and ritual murder. Both, from his point of view, were right and inevitable and we have forfeited the right to do anything about it all. Is that what you implied?

ANSWER

Certainly not. And I wish we could evolve a language in which the word "blame" never appeared! In my view nothing that modern European man has done in Africa justifies the reaction of Mau-Mau on the part of the African. There is a popular notion about that the European has brought nothing but evil to Africa, which is quite untrue. With his vices he brought also his virtues, his great and lasting conscious values. But even if the European were as bad as some people like to think he is that would not justify the African in being worse. European man's injustice in the past does not justify the injured race now repeating the discredited pattern of behaviour which the European himself has already discarded. This would produce a dangerous inertia and evasion of proper responsibilities in the urgent press of events. The trouble again, I believe, is due to our causalistic concept of life, to our linear idea of a chain of cause and effect. This causalistic approach to the mercurial soul and nature of man is dangerously limited. Today even physics is fast abandoning the causal explanation of phenomena and finding the law of cause and effect increasingly inadequate as a basis for describing the eccentric "unlawful" behaviour of matter. It is facing the fact that in the heart of what seems to be a solid, fixed and immutable body, other elements enter and follow their own unpredictable way. In the spirit of man the limitations of the concept are, I believe, far greater. "Cause and effect" are for me only two aspects of something much greater than either, something into which the first is drawn and from which the second flows. They are two terminal points of what I call the "now" of being. The practical consequences of such a belief in our daily thinking would be far-reaching. The moral that flows logically from it is that no matter how great the evil done to us we are not absolved from the responsibility of our reactions. Action and reaction are equals in responsibility to their greater whole for the ensuing result, and the deed of one cannot confer absolution on the other. That, to me, explains the New Testament admonition to "turn the other cheek." I have never been able to believe that that meant that man was not to defend himself against murderers and evildoers and all who come against him with physical force in the physical world. I could never take it to mean, for instance, that the Europeans and Christian Kikuyu in Kenya are wrong in defending themselves against Mau Mau. Christ, I believe, was using an every-day occurrence in the visible world to illustrate a deeper invisible truth. He was telling a world obsessed with Roman faith in power and physical might that, for the truly contemporary man, the man aware of this "now" of being, the Old Testament law of cause and effect, of action and reaction, a blow for a blow, an eye for an eye, a tooth for a tooth and so on, could not apply. The full free spirit must not resist an injury but must accept it as an inevitable aspect of reality. Then, though man be forced to wage war for his preservation in the physical world, he will be saved from carrying the battle over into his own heart and mind. In other words, inflicted injuries are not to be turned into so-called spiritual causes, for by "turning the other cheek" we bring to bear on our injury not the hurt side of ourselves, but a fresh, uninjured aspect not hitherto shown.

It seems so strange that we, who so readily accept the laws of nature in the physical world, should find it so hard to accept that there are natural laws as profound and exacting in the world within. We know that if we ignore the laws of gravity we break our necks. Disaster after disaster in our personal and national lives can only mean that we are flouting laws of the motivating world within us and losing our soul in the process. "Turning the other cheek" is one of these laws, yet we continue to ignore it. To apply this law to our subject matter therefore means that neither Europeans nor Mau-Mau are justified in finding a spiritual basis for future action in the injuries they now inflict or have inflicted on one another. Unless both black and white can learn to see their situation in this new-old way and accept that they

are equally charged with responsibility, there can
be nothing but another dreary round of the already
discredited pattern of social disaster ahead. To be
honest, however, I admit that I put a greater responsibility for what is happening on the white man
than on the black. I do so because the white man
is in active command and is the more conscious of
the two. I believe the positive responsibility must
always lie in the more conscious partner, but that
does not mean that my black countrymen are
without heavy and exacting responsibilities in this
matter.

[...]

QUESTION

I hope you will not think that what I am going to
ask means I underrate the importance of the inner
factors you have outlined for us. But I cannot concur
wholeheartedly in your explanation as to how this
acute state has come about. I cannot accept that it is
mainly induced by what you call European man's
one-sided attitude to himself. That contributes to it,
but it seems to me that other factors are as important. For instance, there is the economic factor,
the fact that the white man in many places has taken
land from the African so that the African often has
not enough land and the white man, comparatively,
too much. There is the fact that the black man is an
easy source of cheap labour and that his existence
enables the white man to have a far higher standard
of living and to live in greater comfort than he could
in Europe. Surely these economic factors are most
important? Yet, except for a perfunctory reference
to them at the beginning of your talk, they play no

role in your considerations. I confess I find this omission puzzling. Could you tell us more about this, please?

ANSWER

Some of us have strange ideas as to what constitutes "higher standards of living." There is a manner wherein the despised bushman living in the Kalahari Desert has a higher standard of living than any of us sitting here. But I hoped I had explained that I left economics out of this talk because, though it can illustrate, it cannot account for what is happening in Africa. I do not mean to imply thereby that economics do not matter. The land problem for the Kikuyu, for instance, is very desperate. In every sense of the word that situation is terribly important, but it is important in a dimension which has no basic application to what we are discussing tonight. If you are curious about its general bearing on events in Africa, you will have no difficulty in satisfying your curiosity, for the libraries of the world are stacked with books by distinguished minds on the subject. These economic factors are the stock-in-trade of every pedlar in patent panaceas for the ills of the world. They provide the first explanation that leaps to our minds, and they would not have side-tracked our energies for so long did they not possess firm roots in reality. I have no wish to decry them or their reality. I only wish them restored to their native proportions. To me, they are not first causes, and I am trying here to outline what seems to me the first causes of African unrest and to discover the master-level where all levels are joined, the centre round which the troubled sphere of our time revolves. And economics I believe plays a part remote from this centre.

For instance, specifically, if you look at the African situation in terms of economics, you will find yourself up against a blank wall. Economically the African indubitably is better off than he has ever been before. His livelihood is more secure, Western science enables him to live longer and breed more prolifically, and Western foresight and knowledge come to his aid in the famines and epidemics which hitherto have destroyed him. He has a larger share of the material goods of this world and what is called a "higher standard of living." It is true he still has far less than the European, but economically his life is definitely on the upgrade. If economics were at the heart of the matter he ought to be well content. If it were true that you make people happier merely by putting more money in their pockets, then the African ought to be increasingly happy. But Africa is not unlike the rest of Europe and the world in this respect. None of us would deny the great material progress made in modern times, nor the security conferred on man by the welfare state. But what of the long shadow thrown by that progress and the great paradox implicit in that security? For who can ignore that far from being increasingly satisfied by these conditions modern man is becoming increasingly restive and his mental and spiritual anxieties daily deepen. He seems to be less and less contained in his own life. His day may be ordered and secure, but his imagination in the stillness of night and the patient, all-absorbent stillness of our aboriginal dark knows only a troubled, hungry, nightmarish rest. Wherever I go in the world I am amazed by the numbers of displaced persons I meet. I do not mean people "displaced" in the obvious sense of having been forced out of their native countries as the Jews were by Nazi Germany or as other peoples were from behind the Iron Curtain. I mean individuals who are displaced in their own native context, individuals who find that the society to which they belong no longer corresponds to their deepest needs, and decreasingly expresses what they most truly are. Indeed, man's feeling of inner insecurity and meaninglessness in this world so uniquely of his own creation seems to have increased in almost direct proportion to the growth of his material security and economic self-importance, and his efforts to break out of this rational, unified social framework to have become correspondingly more violent. Again, I am not saying that the approach to life which has conferred such obvious benefits upon us is wrong and unimportant. All I suggest is that it is *overworked* and made to perform services and satisfy needs that are foreign to it. So economics explains little of African unrest. It is not a first cause but rather one of the mediums through which the invisible potential of man reveals itself, and in which his observance or transgression of the laws of his spirit expresses itself.

An old hunter in Africa, the simplest and wisest man I ever knew, once said to me, "The difference between the white man and the black man in Africa is that the white man 'has' and the black man 'is.'" There in a home-grown nut-shell is the first cause of the trouble as I see it, not only in Africa but in the world, namely, the failure to realize that man "is" before he "has"; that "possession" is no substitute for "being." The greatest economist of our time made his reputation by writing a book called *The Economic Consequences of the Peace*. The book that really needs to be written is "The Economic Consequences of the Nature of Man." For this overworked importance of economics in our values more than any other factor is responsible for the grim shocks that we have had to endure in our relationships with Asiatic and African peoples. I shall never forget a sad, embittered moment after the war when the Dutch leaders in Java realized for the first time that the desire of the Indonesians to see them leave those lovely emerald islands of the East was no passing emotion and that their empire, the third largest in the world, was tumbling down about them. I remember the governor-general turning to me and saying, "I cannot understand it. Look what we have done for them. Look at the schools and the hospitals we have given them. A hundred years ago the population was only a few millions, today it is nearly sixty millions. We have done away with malaria, plague and dysentery and given them a prosperous, balanced economy. Everyone has enough to eat. We have given them an honest and efficient administration and abolished civil war and piracy. Look at the roads, the railways, the industries—and yet they want us to go. Can you tell me why they want us to go?" And I felt compelled to say, "Yes, I think I can: I'm afraid it is because you've never had the right look in the eye when you spoke to them."

It may sound inadequate, but just think, for one moment, of the light that is in the eye of a human being when he looks at another human being he loves and respects as an equal. Then remember the look in the eye of the average European when he is in contact with "a lesser breed without the law," and you will understand what I mean. The difference between the two, I believe, is the explosive that has blown the Europeans out of one country after another during our time.

QUESTION

Mr. Chairman, I beg your pardon but I must protest. I have no such exaggerated and inhuman concept of economics. I was merely trying to find out from the speaker what contribution economics made to the situation in Africa in this predominantly economic world and this increasingly industrialized age. Surely all the trouble cannot be due to what the speaker would call our economic preoccupations?

ANSWER

Of course not. I thought I had explained that. I think the answer is to be found in our general one-sided attitude, in our exaggerated materialism and gross overvaluation of the physical world and of man's achievements in the physical world. It is so because this one-sidedness is a product of long and steady growth. In itself it is not so very reprehensible. It is, after all, the time-honoured way whereby man makes his living and increases his

holding in the black forest and among the blind
forces of nature about him. The trouble only starts
when the process is pushed too far, for then a law of
diminishing returns sets in and threatens the in-
tegrity of man's spirit. Other aspects of man which
have been overlooked and neglected because of this
favouritism towards one part of himself tend to rise
in angry rebellion against him. He is forced then, if
he is not to be torn asunder, to reverse a process
to which he owes much and to suspend a most valu-
able evolutionary trend. This is something which
few individuals and no nation yet seem to have accomplished without the *help* of disaster. Oh, the
phenomenon is not new! The favoured aspect varies
from age to age, but the machinery for this kind
of excess breeding more excess and then begetting
its own vengeful redress, is as old as life itself. It
is a constantly recurring theme in the Greek trage-
dies. Chinese thinking is deeply influenced by it and
expresses the belief that everything in life sooner or
later goes over into its opposite. "At midnight noon
is born," the Chinese proverb says. Thus the legends
and mythology of the world are all full of a submerged warning to man against the danger of in-

definitely exceeding a part of himself at the expense of totality in personality.

There, for instance, we have the key to the significance of the one-eyed giants who stride so strangely through Greek and Roman mythology. I suspect that their gruesome presence there does not mean that a race of one-eyed colossi once walked the earth with seven-leagued strides and brushed the thunder clouds out of their hair. Only on the most elementary and literal levels can they be taken to represent a man grown into monstrous physique with only one eye in the middle of his forehead. But in the aboriginal language of the spirit, in the underlying thought processes of man it is a different and meaningful story, and the giant is the image of a man who has grossly exceeded himself in a part of himself. Only one eye is planted in the cretin head to indicate that he has not the two-way vision that the complete spirit needs but only this one-way look into a world of outward-bound senses. So also the two eyes of contemporary man when they focus *as one* on the outer physical world give him only one-way sight and admit of only one-way traffic. European man is fast forgetting to balance the fixed outward stare with a questioning inward glance, and therein lies our great and growing danger. In the manner immemorial of the spirit this aspect of fundamental meaning is first made accessible to the mind by dramatic personification. The giant and his one eye are projected like an image in a cinema onto the darkened screen of our minds to draw attention to this constantly recurring danger which besets man on his odyssey back from honourable battle in the physical world towards the fulfilment he has earned on the island-self he left behind him when he was young. The poet Blake, too, illustrates and confirms this in a manner closer to our own time. Blake had a uniquely inspired intuition of inner reality. Not only is his poetry full of unconscious truth but also his many canvasses are charged with magnetic personifications of the neglected titans and unused energies in modern man's averted nature. In "The Marriage of Heaven and Hell" he showed an acute awareness of one of the abiding problems of culture in a world "of dark satanic mills," a problem which is inextricably entangled with the situation we are discussing today. He was one of the first to spot the "one-eyed giant" of our time poking his head up above the clear horizon of what was considered to be the beginning of an era of permanent enlightenment and reason. His intuitive awareness of the presence of this danger was so accurate and acute and so in harmony with the aboriginal language of the spirit that he actually wrote of the "one-eyed vision of science." Unfortunately I have no time to go into this fully tonight. I need only stress that the age of one-eyed giants is never over. If they disappear temporarily from one aspect of our being they quickly reappear in another. They are always within us and about us. That is why the story of Odysseus can never lose its freshness. That is why to this day we shiver with apprehension when Cyclops throws Odysseus and his companions into his cave. For we, too, are confined in a cave and threatened with annihilation by the "one-eyed giant" we have made of ourselves and our age. Though our cave is furnished with up-to-date comfort and equipped with all modern conveniences, though it is air-conditioned and bright with electric light, it is an archaic prison of a vital part of ourselves nonetheless. There we are confined by a hungry, tyrannical and cannibal giant. Thus we are sealed off, as Odysseus and his crew were in the cave, from the sun, the moon, the stars. The un-manned ship grates its urgent keel on the yellow foreshore, its sails flap idly in the wind that would carry us home from some warring beachhead in the world without to wholeness with the half we left behind on an island self when young.

So to make this generality of our time specific in the problem at hand I would say, European man has walked into Africa like a one-eyed giant. He has walked into it, moreover, at a moment when he already feels threatened from within. He is instinc-tively aware of danger and takes desperate precau-tions against it, but he takes them in the wrong dimension of reality. He, too, has confused the re-flection of danger within with the mirror without. So he projects his fear of danger onto the black man around him, and this he does all the more read-ily because of the miraculously preserved archaic quality of Africa and the African. So, many of the qualities which the European one-eyed vision de-spises and rejects within himself reappear in the in-digenous society around him. Consequently he en-deavours with increasing desperation to thrust the bearers of his projection back into their cave and

The Discussion

endeavours with laws, regulations and economic barriers to elaborate a new escape-proof prison in which he can safely lock natural African society, believing with fatal naïveté that he is thereby preserving himself and his one-eyed species forever.

QUESTION

I was very interested in what you said previously about the two aspects of man. You said we all had a "dark brother" within, and included the black man, too, when you spoke of the "dark, rejected aspect" within him. Yet surely the side that is rejected in the black man is that personified by the white man? Would it not be better, therefore, to speak of his "rejected white brother" within?

ANSWER

Not entirely. The unlived aspect of man, I believe, always, at a profound level, presents itself in the warning symbolism of the human spirit as a dark being. That is one of the reasons why I reminded you earlier on of the fact that when the white sun of pure reason blazed at its fiercest in France the alarm was sounded in the intuitive mind of Rousseau and he was driven to express it as a rationalized concern for the natural spirit of man in his concept of a noble *savage,* of a noble dark being. You will find an awareness of the same rejected reality in your poets and artists. There was de Nerval, for instance, whose imagination was as submerged in the rejected being of his day as the lobster he led on a ribbon through the streets of Paris once was in the sea. There was his poem about his dark hero "Le Prince d'Aquitaine a la tour abolie." There was Andrew Lang's translation in England of this poem and the significant line, "that dark, that disinherited, that all dishonoured son of Aquitaine." There is the same intuitive awareness in Rimbaud which sharpened his spirit prepared to slam the shutters on the inward preoccupations of his genius. More significantly still there is after Rimbaud's rejection of his conscious self this strangely logical turning of his to the dark continent. They and many others have compelled the imaginations of even the most rational and intellectual among us because there is this dark, abolished, and in its turn abolishing aspect in all of us. It was this warning aspect which towards the end of the eighteenth century and throughout the nineteenth motivated the growing interest and concern for the dark children of the world, led to the abolition of slavery and the great missionary ef-

fort in Africa. Your question, therefore, suggests to
me that you may have been caught up in one of
the basic confusions which make relationships between black and white so baffling and painful. You
confuse two different levels of reality. You assume
that because the black African has a black skin that
he has a "black being" and vice versa with the European. In other words you confuse "colour" in its
aboriginal and abiding language of the spirit with
its literal meaning. That is precisely what my countrymen in South Africa do and up to a point it was,
perhaps, a pardonable error. Nonetheless, the black
man in Africa does not feel himself to be black. He
feels himself to be as filled with whiteness as we do.
He too stains the white radiance of eternity like a
dome of many-coloured glass until death tramples
him to fragments. Black in this ancient language of
the spirit has precisely the same meaning for him
that it has for us and the colour of a man's skin is
not the colour of his being. To this day when the
Zulus speak of their tragic tyrant Chaka they say,
"But auck! He had a black heart," just as the European when speaking of a good fellow calls him "a
white man," both instinctively making the vital differentiation between inner and outer "whiteness"

and "blackness." For example, I seldom turn on a radio nowadays without hearing an American singer complaining that he is "blue," yet I do not for a moment therefore imagine that America is inhabited by blue as well as red Indians!

One of the more sinister symptoms of the pathological state of mind of my own people is that today they seem to have become incapable of this simple but vital differentiation in regard to their black countrymen. They are, therefore, quite terrified of "going black" themselves. I suggest that the blackness which they fear is not the colour in the African skin without but rather the nature of their own inner darkness. Could they but separate, emotionally, these two dimensions in "colour" and realize that the tide of "colour," the blackness which threatens their civilization, is largely within themselves, I am certain that colour prejudice would quickly lose its point and all the illusory defensive values attached to it disappear.

At the same time I must admit that when you spoke of the "white aspect of the black man," you brushed up against something else of great importance. I suspect that among many black Africans there is an instinctive fear of "going white" in the inner sense and that this fear plays its part in the problem we are discussing. I believe that this fear of "going white" exists at a certain level in all of us. It is the fear that man has of becoming more conscious, of becoming more aware of himself, of detaching himself from the herd and assuming greater responsibility for himself and his actions. For greater consciousness is not attained without effort, pain and added responsibility and is maintained only by a continuous struggle. If this fear exists in modern civilized man, as I believe it does, it is even more active in primitive communities.

We ourselves have gone so far along the uphill road of consciousness that we have forgotten what the journey cost us. Our conscious achievements stretch behind us like a view from the battlements of a great fortress. We no longer remember the great dangers overcome, the frequent loss of soul and disappearance into the oblivion of outer darkness of those who have brought us to this fortified point. Until war or sudden social and individual disaster penetrates our conscious defences we see only the glittering civilized and defended scene lying below and before us. Primitive man, however, is still near the bottom of the hill. His life still derives meaning from memory of the locked lagoon of his pre-conscious state. Of the new road ahead he knows only few advantages to set against abundant peril. Anyone who would entice him further along this new road, therefore, arouses the fiercest resistance and provokes in him the greatest conflict and fear. The coming of European man with his relatively advanced and sharply focused consciousness inevitably stimulates this sort of conflict and fear within African society to an abnormal degree.

I am certain that I need not stress to you here how real the fear and conflict within the mind and lives of primitive people can be in such circumstances. Only I question how far any of us are capable of sharing in its overwhelming emotions. Until we ourselves are in the absolute power of a people with a culture which despises and rejects our own values we cannot understand fully the cruelties, the crippling injury of spirit and the fundamental dishonour that African societies and other less advanced peoples in the world have had to endure from being forced into contact with us. When I was a prisoner of war under the Japanese I was subjected to the rule of a people with a consciousness dominated by a radically different form of awareness from my own.

The situation was sufficiently analogous to add to my understanding of the problems of my black countrymen. Our prison rulers did not speak our language, so they seldom spoke to us and only then through woefully inadequate interpreters. We had no rights, privileges, and no security. Even the fact that we were alive was held to be a shameful argument against us, proof of our guilt and culpability as well as proof of the unprecedented magnanimity of our captors. What we stood for was condemned in advance not because of anything we had done but because of *what we were imagined to be.* None of us stood out as an individual and we were merely a collective reality for our rulers. Often as I tried to prevent a Japanese sentry from ill-treating one of my men for some trivial offence unwittingly committed, I would see a strangely recognizable look on the face and in the eyes of the tortured English, Dutch or Australian soldiers. Where had I seen it before? Then one day I had it. I realized, ashamed, that I had been familiar with that expression all my life and had seen it countless times on the faces of black Africans as they were being belaboured and upbraided by a white employer, or else stood in the dock for trial under a law which was not theirs and

131

in a language that they did not know. I realized then with a bitter emotion that the black man is a prisoner in our world and we a kind of Japanese jailer.

Nor should we forget that there were races in the world which vanished, not because of the wars we waged against them, but simply because contact with us was more than their simple natural spirit could endure. It is almost as if an advanced consciousness has a fatal radioactive quality about it, an ectoplasmic glitter that hypnotizes primitive man out of the ability to be himself and so, logically, he dies. I have time to give only one illustration drawn from the simplest level of my experience to try and show you how easily natural man can be "unselved," to use Gerard Manley Hopkins' telling word, by contact with others more conscious than himself.

Not long ago I came across a party of bushmen deep in the Kalahari. They had never seen white people before and as they mingled with my party in my camp I noticed a curious fact: they seemed compelled to do whatever we were doing. If we got up, they got up; if one of us moved, the bushman watching him would move, too; if one of us eased his hat on his forehead, the bushman opposite him put up his hand and eased a hat that was not there. Now, we had a very distinguished man in our party, a fine-looking person with an impressive head and naturally dignified bearing. The leader of the bush-men gaily attached himself to this man as if it were his natural right, but soon a remarkable change set in in the little yellow man. A curious trancelike ex-pression appeared on his face. Suddenly, just as the great man had given him a cigarette and lit one himself, I saw the little bushman imitating our great man, puffing when he puffed, removing the cigarette from his mouth when the other did in exactly the same way, and soon the yellow man had become so identified with the white man that he had no ges-tures of his own left. In some peculiar way he had become the quintessence of the great man and was almost more like a European than the European was himself. This went on for some while and then the bushman began to struggle with himself like some-one in a nightmare. He looked wildly about him, cut the air between him and the European with two clenched, desperate hands, and in this way broke the spell. Then, realizing what had happened to him, he collapsed onto the sand shaking with laughter. But I noticed afterwards that the confiding manner with which he had attached himself to the white person had gone, that he gave the magnetic man only fearful sidelong glances and kept well away from him.

Now this is an instance of the psychic danger and fear in their most amusing and simplest form. But the primitive African has this very real fear of losing his own unique spirit, and I think it greatly to the credit of both the white and the black man that, so far, the two extremes of hypnotic paralysis and war of extinction have been avoided. Only it does not mean that in between these extremes there is not an area of terrible stress and strain for both sides concerned. One of the most pathetic illusions of the European in Africa is his assumption that he has influenced the black man in Africa but that the black man has not affected him. He regards his life there as a matter largely of one-way traffic, but it is not so. It is an urgent two-way stream for all his illusions to the contrary. All that has happened is that because he despises consciously what Africa has to give, Africa bestows its dynamic gifts dangerously and unconsciously, slipping them in through a back door of the spirit where they become nourishment of his own insurgent nature within. The presence of the natural without stimulates the natural within;

the primitive around him excites the primitive within. The inner conflict sharpens, the fear of the rising tide of blackness deepens and the two demonic fears, the fear of "going black" and fear of "going white" bedevil the situation for both races, feeding and growing monstrous on each other and contributing equally with a deadly, impersonal partiality to their common doom.

QUESTION

I find it increasingly difficult to follow Colonel van der Post's use of the term "consciousness." I wonder if he would explain his use of the term before going on. At many points he seemed to me to equate the black man not only with our dark selves but with our unconscious and with unconsciousness. That says to me only one thing: the black man must be incapable of conscious or rational thought.

ANSWER

You know your question is a rather remarkable illustration of how deep down this confusion of the image reflected in the mirror with the mirror itself goes into all of us. For that I fear is at the root of the difficulty behind your question. Of course I do not equate the black man with our own or any other state of unconsciousness. In so far as I talk of the primitive man's unconsciousness I do so relatively. I do not mean that he has no consciousness and is

incapable of rational thought. That would be both
a nonsense and an untruth; some of the most conscious individuals and finest natural intelligences I
have encountered in my life have been among black
countrymen of mine. So when I speak of the unconsciousness of primitive man I speak in a generality to
which there are many striking exceptions already,
but I have to do so. I do so because unsatisfactory as
it may be I do not know of any better way of describing the difference which undoubtedly exists between indigenous and European societies in Africa.
But it is a difference only of degree and it is this
difference which makes the black man so readily a
symbol for the white man of what is unconscious in
himself. I repeat a symbol, because you see I do not
equate the black man, as you put it, with the white
man's unconscious. I merely suggest that his extra
degree of unconsciousness and his more natural and
organic behaviour make him a living mirror in which
the white man sees reflected his own rejected and
abhorred unconscious natural self. Like the baboon,
the white man is incapable of differentiating between the mirror and his own reflection in the
mirror. In the process he is burdening the black man
with a despised and hidden aspect of himself. But

that does not prevent the black man, like the mirror, from having a shape, a being and validity all his own. That shape, I cannot emphasize enough, does not exclude consciousness. On the contrary, because consciousness in it has not yet been separated from its deep and vital instinctive roots, as it increasingly is in the European in Africa, it has access to great power and is blessed with the promise of profound increase.

QUESTION

I am a student of colonial history and I have a difficulty of my own over what Colonel van der Post
has told us. He has mentioned twice "the readiness
to serve" of the African and discussed what he calls
a period of "hush," of "suspended indigenous being"
in Africa. Now I just can't think of these things
historically. I think instead of Kaffir wars, Zulu
wars, rebellions, broken treaties, treachery, riots and
strikes. Then when he goes further and talks of this
period of the "hush" as something which happened
not at the first meeting of white and black far back,
but in his lifetime as well, I just can't fit it all in with
what I know of history.

ANSWER

You are right in one superficial sense, of course.
There was trouble, too, when white and black first
met in Africa. I acknowledged as much myself
earlier on. There has been trouble since. There were

some wars, an odd rebellion or two, a few riots and occasionally a halfhearted strike, particularly in Southern Africa where the contact between white and black is oldest and where the picture has been at its most sombre. But even there I am amazed how little the trouble on the surface has been and how soon after the white man's first determined thrust into the interior, war and rebellion vanished from the land. Of course, again I spoke relatively and not absolutely, and when you consider the history of Africa in relation to that of other countries; when you compare such trouble as there has been with what happened, for instance, between Europeans and Red Indians in the Americas, or for that matter, between European and European at the same time in Europe, you will see at once how little it was. I can think of as many unsavoury exceptions to the general rule as you can, I am sure, but my reading of history and my experience of contemporary equivalents in other parts of the world leave me continually amazed at the initial readiness of the African to accept the European and to follow him. And once you move north of the Limpopo to look into the history of the scattered outposts of the British forming small white islands in the great black continent, the measure and manner of the acceptance become even more striking.

Allow me to give you one more instance of what I meant. During the war I had to take trains of camels loaded with vital war supplies by a back-door route through the Italian lines into Abyssinia. My camel-men were all Sudanese civilians organized in little family and village groups, each under its own headman. I had very definite orders not to take them into the battle areas, but to send them back with their camels once I reached the great Abyssinian escarpment. There I was promised I would find mules and muleteers to take us up into the hills and on to our operational areas. But when I got to the escarpment there were no mules or muleteers. We were desperately needed at the front and we had no option but to disobey our orders. I had no means of forcing my civilian camel-men to accompany me with their camels. I could only ask them to go on with me, and even my right of persuasion seemed poor enough when I saw them ill and shivering in their torn cotton smocks designed for the hot desert climate, round their fires in the keen uplands air. Nevertheless, I gathered them round me and explained the situation to them. I have never forgotten one old headman, who, on his own initiative, addressed the gathering with such eloquence that the issue was settled there and then. He ended up by saying, "Effendi, we have come far with you. We are ill. We are cold. Our feet are tired, and we are covered in sores. But I am older than these other men here. I can remember how it was here before the Government came. If the Government would want us to go on, then we will go on."

"Before the Government came," or its equivalent, I have found all over great tracts of Africa, was the expression used to denote the time before the European came. I could give you many other examples drawn from my own experience of life in rural Africa, and from the history of my own family, but I hope you will trust this incident to speak for them all. It is precisely the existence of this mood of acceptance and preparedness on the part of indigenous Africa, after its first light brush with the invading European, which makes what we are doing in Africa today so disgraceful and so mysterious. Yes, so mysterious—let us be quite clear on this issue. Your question and the manner in which it is framed is an illustration of how terribly one-sided is the conventional historical approach to the problem in

Africa, and how inadequately its conclusions explain our present situation. The history you quote neither resolves the mystery, nor justifies the disgrace. The situation, as I see it, is at once before and beyond history. It is high time we freely cut our umbilical cord with the past in our thinking about the problem in Africa, or disaster will soon do it for us. It is time we stopped using history either as a justification for evading the unpleasant task of accepting the present as our sole responsibility, or as an excuse for doing something disreputable to our neighbours. The history of war and rebellion and broken treaty and treachery is not at the root of our present problems in Africa. We have to look for it nearer and deeper than that, and you know by now, I hope, where I think we have to look.

Then you ask how I can speak of this period of "the hush," of "suspended indigenous being," as something which happened in my lifetime when your history tells you it cannot be so. You must look to your history for yourself. I can only repeat, I spoke as I did because I have experienced this period of "the hush" all over Africa. It is not a matter of history for me but of living experience. What is more, though times have changed and are still changing fast in that respect, it is not yet altogether gone. "The moment of innocence," as I have called it elsewhere, is not altogether spent. I know you may find it hard to believe when you study your latest newspaper, but come with me into rural Africa, away from the few industrial clusters that shine like imitation jewelry strung on a thread of barbaric copper round the vast body of Africa, and you will be amazed to see how much of it still exists in spite of your history. For instance, I have only recently done a long journey through South, Central and East Africa, and everywhere I asked my black country-men if they thought this moment of innocence and opportunity had vanished for good. Many said it had, but very many more said no, said in fact, "It is not too late yet, but we have no time to lose."

QUESTION

I was impressed by what Colonel van der Post said about mythology and its bearing on the events of our time, and also by what he said about the human spirit ceasing to be contemporary and falling back in time. He mentioned the mythology which captured the German imagination as a dark prelude to war. Could he say something more about that and what would he say is the mythology active in Africa today?

ANSWER

I would like to make it clear that I have no pretensions to being an historian. But there is this to be said for me, I have read history with a hunger which to this day is still unsatisfied. My impression is that history describes and accounts for almost everything except its own underlying processes. Always in the deep core of history there seems to preside an invisible presence, a sort of extraterritorial power of which the traditional historian is largely unaware.

It is as if below the opaque field on which events crowd, like black iron filings on a table in an experimental laboratory of physics, an unseen force moves from time to time like a magnet, concentrating and compelling the metal units above it into a vital magnetic pattern. History describes faithfully what happens on the surface of the table, but what goes on underneath remains often beneath its notice. So in the conscientiously recorded history of my own country, South Africa, there are events which are admirably described but never explained. For example, there is the Great Trek. History marshals many causes to account for it. Yet if none of them had existed the Great Trek, I am convinced, would have taken place all the same, because already it was active in the minds and hearts of my countrymen long before it happened in the visible world, just as it still continues to exist inside them to this day. D'Annunzio taunted the science of his day with the reproach that it presupposed a corpse. History, too, presupposes a dead past and historians continue to confuse the dead skin of discarded events in which history dresses itself with the living spirit that has wriggled out of it and moves on, so missing altogether the element which gives history its being

and makes it also a "now." Far back in my life I
seem to have been conscious of an unseen presence
in the history of my people, a strange dreamlike element in the life of those round me which amounted
almost to a sleep-walker's affliction. As I grew older
I realized that the history that mattered in my own
country was not history as it was recorded but as it
was imagined and shaped in accordance with the
laws of some unexplained inner necessity. I saw the
pressures exerted by this unseen factor grow so great
that men were drawn to falsify their written histories in order to justify consciously the behaviour
into which this unknown element blindly compelled
them, and the process continues to this day. It has
an undeniably tragic side, only what is of immediate
point is not the pity of it but the fact that this process seems to confirm the existence and to demonstrate the power of an unrecognized historical dominant.

Now what precisely is this historical dominant? I
can only tell you what I believe it to be: a mythological ingredient in the heart of all our matter; a
mighty mythological activity in the spirit of man.
I believe it to be man's sense not only of the letter
but also of the spirit of his original contract and

charter with life, the keeper within him of life's wider plan. If man is at one with its terms in his conscious striving, it raises him to great heights. If he is separated from it by the presumptions of his daily self, then this mythological factor within him turns into an archaic force which blindly dominates him, using its great strength on him like a giant. There is an old Arab saying: "Tell me what a man dreams and I'll tell you what he is." I would suggest another: "Tell me what is the myth within history that is seeking to express itself through the life of a nation and I'll tell you what that nation is and may become."

You reminded me that I mentioned German mythology. I did so because I believe Germany has given us the supreme example in our day of what happens when an unrecognized mythological activity overtakes a people and has its way with them. Of course, there is also a long and complex history to the German situation, but at heart I would sum it up thus: there has always existed in the German spirit a hard mythological core with which the national character has never squared its accounts; an ancient, neglected racial deposit which has always defied sublimation. For it is a remarkable fact that whereas all Germany's neighbours dissolved and re-formed themselves into the classical and Christian moulds with which they came into living contact, there remained deep in the German spirit an archaic core which resisted outward change and resignation. As the visible "modern" Germany began to take shape, as the Electorate of Brandenburg became the kingdom of Prussia and Prussia became the German Empire, as one by one the outposts of the classical world beyond the Rhine fell and Germany at last acquired power (as for long she had been possessed of the secret will), so we find the impatient mythological energy which had piled up for centuries within its ancient and secret centre of resistance streaming out fast and furious into every nook and cranny of "modern" German spirit.

Let us take for illustration the work of a single individual and examine the whole unconscious conflict making strange old-new music in the prophetic talent of one man of genius. I wonder if any of you have ever thought what a terrible portent the music of Wagner is? I never listen to it without feeling I need to cross myself. For me the whole process we have been discussing reveals itself in this tidal music. Here is not a mythological theme freely chosen and put to conscious use, but, on the contrary, here mythology chooses a composer and swings his talent like a swollen sea to its own secret will. Here not only the theme but the music itself is sheer mythology. I recognize that Wagner made his own heroic effort to transcend this conflict in the unlived collective spirit of his race. I remember that besides *Siegfried* and the *Götterdämmerung* there are also *Lohengrin* and *Parsifal.* But in his music one is forever conscious of the angry moon-swung waters rising fast and pounding against the leaking dykes in the mind of individual man. It makes great equinoctial music, but for all that it is tribal music; it is perhaps the greatest tribal music ever written. I have heard the same rhythms on the drums of Africa and encountered the same compulsions in the African music which accompanies the ritual designed to overcome the last conscious human resistances and to bring about the unconditional surrender of the individual self to an unconscious tribal fate. And in Germany, barely a generation after Wagner, we had proof absolute of how this power of which I have spoken works within us before it becomes visible without. "I go the way fate has pointed me as assuredly as a man walking in his

sleep," Hitler said at this stage, describing the
nightmare state in which they all moved far more
accurately than he or the frantic millions who ap-
plauded him could ever know. There was no Parsifal
left in the music of the German nation as it swelled
to its final crescendo, but only the twilight of gods,
only the doomed herds on one side of the gulf and
on the other the forces of darkness massing at the
foot of the rainbow bridge. The split which would
not close itself, the cleft spirit that would not freely
mend the breach between its origin and destination
was ready for delivery into the hands of the im-
placable healer, disaster. However, I need not ana-
lyze for you how the receding German mind from
1914 to 1939 went further and further back and
over its age-long trail like a bloodhound that has lost
the scent of blood. The individual humanistic values
which European man had evolved for himself at
such painful cost were overthrown. The impersonal,
inhuman concepts of the herd took over, and values
that one thought permanently discredited, hoary
and senile with antiquity, were installed. Indeed,
things happened then in Europe which make it
quite impossible for me to have any privileged feeling of horror over what is happening in Africa today.

However, this unresolved mythological element working in nations like a great volcano stirring from sleep does appear to me to have certain recognizable "symptoms" which are perhaps worth mentioning. Firstly, nations in this state seem to avoid accepting full responsibility for their national condition because it is too great and painful a burden, and then blame their defects and shortcomings on others. They are, in that respect, like a person who has had an unhappy childhood and goes on using the conflict between his parents as an excuse for his own imperfections of character, not realizing that he cannot be a mature human being until he has accepted the parental conflict and all his past as a part of his own nature and character. Another characteristic of nations which are nursing a secret mythological content is the conviction that they are pledged on pain of extermination to this overwhelming cosmic secret and are utterly different from other men. Yes, this feeling of possessing a vital secret works in them as an unconfessable secret works in the individual. It isolates them and sets them fatally apart from other men, so depriving them of the healing, instinctive communion with the society of life, and condemning them to a form of exile which is all the more terrible because it presupposes an absence of all desire for return. Such lean and hungry nations are dangerous both to themselves and to those that are fat and sleep well of nights. Through the tranced, mediumistic concentration of purpose which exile of this kind imposes on their imagination and will, they acquire a terrible inhuman power over themselves and others. The final effect on a nation of a mythological content which is not related to the general trend and demands of the age is that the nation comes to assume it has been selected by life for a special task and has superior sanction for its differences with other nations. All these elements compose in their most primitive *individual* form the myth of the hero or Superman. In their most primitive *collective* form they compose the myth of the superior race or God-chosen people.

And here I come at last to your question: what myth is active in Africa today? I would say that under all the many and various outer forms in which you encounter it, there is only one really predominant myth which by positive assertion or negative induction sets the fashion for all the others. It is the myth of the European of Africa, and this is precisely the myth which Europe fought so hard to defeat and eliminate in Germany: the myth of the superior race. Among my own people, the Afrikaners, this myth goes far beyond the comparatively civilized evaluations of racial superiority and emerges from a profound level as the fanatical myth of a God-chosen people. This explains the extraordinary sympathy the Afrikaner in Africa has always had for Germany and why his imagination has become increasingly allied to the pre-war German thinking. There are historians who would say that the whole thing was started by a telegram the last German Kaiser sent to Paul Kruger. Or they argue that it was hatred and fear of Britain that drove the Afrikaner to side with Germany. All these things have their own importance but underneath it there is something else. The Afrikaner recognizes intuitively that the myth which impelled pre-war Germany "as assuredly as a man walking in his sleep" is not unlike the one that seems to him to give direction and meaning to his own presence in Africa. All he has lacked in Africa is the sheer physical power which would have enabled him to abandon himself to the practice and pursuit of this myth of a superior race as wholeheartedly as the Germans did in Europe. If one were guided by rational historical facts one might have expected exactly the opposite. One might have imagined, for instance, that when Germany so brutally overran Holland the Afrikaners would have been overcome with horror and indignation. But, on the contrary, most of them digested the unpalatable fact without difficulty. Some of their leaders even went so far as to express their opinion that it served their ancestral country right for standing in the way of this masterful new Germany!

No, so irrational a reaction can only have an irrational explanation. I believe that, by and large, it is due to the fact that in their deeps the two nations for a moment had come to share a myth and recognized in each other an archaeopteryx of the same prehistoric feather. The outward fact that the country which finally arrested Germany's advance was the same liberal Britain which so often had crossed their path in Africa merely confirmed for the Afrikaners the rightness of their inward point of departure. And as their power has increased since the war so the similarity to the pre-war Germany accordingly has become daily more obvious, not only in their bearing but also in a growing love for mass celebration and herd occasions, and in the curiously primitive, almost mystical exaltation and belligerence which overwhelms them wherever they collect in crowds. Even more striking is the parallel with pre-war German political thinking. In my country there is the same steady elimination of individual values and rights and the same arbitrary collective standards put in their place as there was in Germany between wars. There is the same transformation of racial prejudices into legal imperatives; the same mounting hatred of the white-skinned Aryan for the dark non-Aryan breeds; the same absence of self-criticism and the same sensitiveness and intolerance to the criticism of others; the same conviction of unique national rightness and the same capacity for feeling misunderstood; the same exaltation of the state at the expense of the individual; and the same assertion of a *droit collectif* over the principle of the rule of law and the concern for the individual that goes with it.

Not long ago I was in one of the university towns in my country and while I was there the political head of the state came to address the university. He read a long, involved, earnest lecture on how the task of the true university was to serve the state with all its mind and all its heart. At the finish he received prolonged ecstatic applause which turned my blood cold, for it was a sound I myself had never heard in my own country before. The last time I had heard it was at a Hitler rally at Nuremberg. After the applause the young fell into obedient, automatic ranks and marched out of sight behind standards bearing portraits of their distinguished visitor over the slogan: "You lead and youth follows." How often has one not seen the same scene enacted in Germany? I thought of Grey of Fallodon in August of 1914 saying, "The lamps are going out all over Europe." I thought of my people then and now, only forty years later; they no longer seem the same people to me. One by one the ancient proved lamps of the spirit that had brought us through the dark of our heroic past, were being put out in my country, too, with always an excellent reason, a high-minded argument or an admirable moral plea to justify it.

The Discussion

QUESTION

I take it then that you believe that what is happening in Africa today is entirely due to Germany's influence and bad example?

ANSWER

Thank you for the question because without it we might not have understood each other. The answer is no, I do not believe it. I believe that what is happening in Africa is in this particular sense quite independent of anything that has happened in Europe. The resemblances that I have tried to outline are fundamental but there exist differences, too, at least one of which is extremely important. The mythological pattern which overwhelmed the conscious German spirit was essentially pagan, but the myth which dominates the history of my country is the myth of the God-chosen race as revealed in the Holy Bible. It is not pagan. It is not necessarily pre-doomed to outer darkness as was the ancient

German myth. Remember that for generations the Bible was the only book my countrymen ever read. Because of it many of them were persecuted in Europe and driven into exile in Africa, and in *The Book* they found their inspiration and comfort. They came out of Europe like the Israelites out of bondage in Egypt to search for their promised land. Unless you have lived the pattern with them as I have, you cannot know how deeply the Old Testament example was burnt into them and how unfailingly the experience thrust on them by Africa seemed to confirm their own affinity with the Biblical story. Even the first book written in Afrikaans argued that the original garden of Eden was in the heart of Africa. To this day Africa is largely an Old Testament land which still needs temples and prophets and a David for Goliath far more than it needs parliaments, politicians and trade unions. Three hundred years ago when my people first went there, Africa fitted their Old Testament myth like a glove. That is why I said to you just now that if none of the causes historians elicit to explain the Great Trek existed, it would have happened nonetheless. This particular myth of my countrymen presupposed just such a journey as the Great Trek through a great

unknown wilderness to a land of promise. It was a
necessary and inevitable phase in the development
of their myth. But if today this Old Testament myth
seems to be perilously receding, it is because it is
still confined in its Old Testament context and has
never been finally transcended into New Testament
teaching and example. This brings me to a point I
believe is vital. No living myth can be pinned down
to one particular phase of its inherent development
or to one consciously selected and favoured aspect
of itself. It, too, is a moving finger that writes and,
having written, moves on. If we deny it its onward
movement it will go back and rewrite the lesson on
the rough blackboard of life with some extra lines
on disaster thrown in after school hours. It works in
this way because it contains the great rounded
vision of life without bias, fear or favour for any of
its parts. It has the power to accomplish the vision
in full and the will to insist that life shall be lived
in its entirety. It is a law in itself, too, which life
cannot oppose without destroying itself and to which
its being is subject just as inanimate matter is subject to gravity. I know of no history which is immune to it and no race which has escaped it. Ob-
viously, therefore, the ways in which it announces

itself, and the terms on which its unfailing energies
are placed at the disposal of the spirit of man, are as
many and varied as life itself. But one time-honoured
myth is that in which man is chosen and called upon
to perform "a perilous journey." It is this myth, of
course, which is so utterly transcended and accomplished in the New Testament. This is also the myth
which rules in the hearts of my countrymen. Only
since it has not yet been transcended because the
European in Africa at the moment will not carry
it forward, and since by the laws of its own dynamic
being it cannot stand still, inevitably it has begun to
recede and an earlier pattern, a less conscious phase
of it, begun to replace a more conscious one.

The Discussion

QUESTION

But is there then no way in which such a recession of man's spirit as you describe can be prevented?

ANSWER

Before all else we must learn to read the language of the myth not merely in one but in all its living dimensions. If we interpret it only in terms of the physical world it remains merely a difficult journey on a geographical plain undertaken on promise of inordinate privilege denied to other men. That, however, is the meaning of the myth in only its kindergarten preliminaries. This element in man as keeper of the vision of life in all its fullness and triumphant wholeness is ultimately concerned with a journey of a different kind. It is concerned with a journey made not on foot nor by donkey, camel, horse, oxwagon, ship or aeroplane, but a journey from one state of being to another, a journey of *becoming*. It

is the Far Journey of which the great Yu Ching
spoke:

> And the deeper secret within the secret:
> The land that is nowhere, that is the true home.

The race impelled to undertake the Far Journey
in this other living dimension is not exclusively
Greek, Roman, Jewish, German or Afrikaner. The
varying races are used to indicate the fact that the
myth begins with a state of being that we know, and
the inadequacy of this state of being is symbolized
by the trials and persecutions, the years in bondage or captivity in the physical world to which it is
subjected. The feeling that the person or race is
superior to the subordinations of the physical world,
that it is indeed God-chosen, is a sign of reassur-
ance that the person or race possesses the power to
undertake and accomplish the journey however impossible and difficult it may appear. The journey itself is not a mere changing of place, an exchange of
geographical locations, but a change of being, a becoming, the task indeed of travelling from the
familiar being man receives from his parents to the
distant being he has neither known nor seen in this
other invisible dimension of the spirit. The golden

fleece, the jewel at the bottom of the distant well, reunion in Ithaca, the promised land on the other side of the great desert, are one and all symbols of the brave new being with which the journeyman who has travelled the whole way with his myth is rewarded.

If you examine the history of my countrymen by this light, I believe you will see how truly they have lived out the opening phases of their myth. They have responded heroically to the call for the first stage of the journey in the dangerous Old Testament world of Africa. In fact they have lived it out so fully that they are now standing face-to-face with the new central act of their inner drama, and are confronted with the same challenge and choice of ways which once presented itself to another God-chosen race, the Jews in the New Testament. My countrymen, too, are now called upon to move out of the physical plane of their journey and to carry it on into the mind and spirit. They are now called upon to free themselves from the Egypt of their worldly senses, from captivity in the Babylon of their outer histories, and to carry the myth forward into a realm where race and physical being have no automatic privileged meaning, but where kinship is determined by the deeper and abiding considerations of life for all those who, whatever their colour or race, have answered the ancient challenge and have committed themselves to the "journey of becoming."

I am sure I need not stress to you that this is exactly what the New Testament did to the Old. It freed the Hebraic myth from racial bondage as the Israelites were freed from Egypt, destroyed its limited meaning and carried it forward into a wider nonracial validity.* It opened thereby a whole new continent to the spirit of man and discovered a far greater new world than ever did Columbus or any sailor of the seven seas. But it is an obvious symptom of our one-eyed vision and our crippling preoccupation with the physical world that geographical discovery has continued to excite our imagination more than the inner realities of this other great world of adventure. No wonder, therefore, that so far my countrymen, too, have shirked crossing the frontier and have turned their backs on the line of their advance as did the Jews on Christ and His apostles. They, too, cling to the literal truth of the word and

---

* The fact that the Jews themselves rejected the forward movement of their own myth adds to the irony but does not detract from the validity of the New Testament event.

power of the law in utter incomprehension of the
alchemy of forgiveness and quicksilver transcendence of power in love, just as the Jews once clung to
their ancient concepts of an eye for an eye and a
tooth for a tooth, and of a superior race favoured by
God and of lesser breeds destined to be but hewers
of wood and drawers of water. In consequence, the
tide of my countrymen's myth has begun to ebb in
them and threatens to leave them stranded on the
bleak island shore of their histories, like that lone
survivor of Odysseus' crew encountered by Aeneas
on the island of one-eyed giants.

You may argue that men all over the world are
doing the same sort of thing. Yet if you carefully consider the short history of my country this condition
represents a stark and terrifying decline. For you
must realize that the individuals who comprised the
first European community in Africa were all drawn
from nations in the van of the rediscovery of the un-
exhausted potentialities and untapped vitalities of
the Christian myth. They were in the forefront of
that movement to free the individual from totali-
tarianism of the spirit and fascist domination of the
mind, which we call the Reformation. They were
identified with the movement of man to accept sole

responsibility of himself before God and then, the mystery of things full upon him, pledged to make a new being out of his ancient leaden self. The conviction of having been chosen for such a task sustained the individual through the ensuing persecutions and sent him out of his familiar context in the physical world to resume his unfinished journey. When these people first came to Africa three hundred years ago they were approaching the New Testament transformation of their myth. Yet the God that is worshipped today has declined in stature and become an exacting tribal god, a touchy racial spirit, the terrible and infinitely jealous Jehovah of my Afrikaner people; and when the gods decline nations wither; when they die civilizations die with them.

It seems that it is not enough that a man should be born of his time; his mature, his Odyssean task is to make his being of his time. Here, too, we have to think on more than one level. Here there is the literal physical level of the one-eyed tyrant and the other deeper inner dimension which transcends it. On the first level we are all modern people belonging to our own time; but at the deeper level few of us are more than partially modern. Most of us are of our time almost in a technical sense only; we use

rather than serve it. The time of day and the time
our being keeps, calendar and inner time, are often
eras apart. How rare it is to meet a spirit that will
give life its full 1954 meaning. Twentieth-century
man in one profound sense has not yet been born.
We have seen in our age a world-wide revolt of man
against the vested economic interests and privileges
derived from a discarded past. What we still have
not realized is that there are vested interests of the
mind and spirit, tyrannies and despot tracts of
knowledge and history, that hem us in and stand
between us and our twentieth-century experience
and meaning. We are like a profoundly preoccupied
person limping painfully along the highway of being, not noticing that he has his bread-and-butter
foot on the "Anno Domini" pavement while his
other mythological foot still drags in some B.C. gut-
ter. Few individuals and still fewer nations, I believe, are capable of being "of their time" in both dimensions. Very few of us can see and accept the demands and necessities of our age as a problem of
unrealized being in ourselves. There is in most of us
a dark gap between what we are and what we are
challenged to be, and only the myth, like a bloodhound on our trail, can drive us into bridging the

distance. It is exactly this agonizing awareness of
the time-lag in himself which is responsible for
Hamlet's cry of despair: "The time is out of joint:
Oh! cursed spite! that ever I was born to set it right."
On one level he is the envied heir to royalty, with
love and honour beckoning closely to him. On the
other level he is not of his time at all but is living far
back in an archaic world of ancient fate, his spirit
imprisoned in a deep oubliette made of the secret
knowledge of patricide, with the sense of his mother's guilt an unforgiving jailer that will not release
his emotions for Ophelia and his own bright day.
We continue to weep with Hamlet because our time,
too, is terribly out of joint. One way or another we,
too, are in a dungeon of secret awareness of crime,
of a failure in being to match the vital challenge of
our time. Though we continue to tell the time of day
by calendar and clock, this other unsynchronized
Hamlet is within us, with this guilt which is a sense
of the inadequacy of the countries that mother us.*

---

* Our countries in the aboriginal language of the spirit, of
course, are parents to us. I believe there is a significant clue to a
nation's character in the way it thinks of its parent country:
whether it thinks of it as a father or a mother country. Germany
is perhaps the most striking example of a father country; Japan is
another, and for both, as if in conformance to the law of the
great opposites, the sun, which combines with the country to

We can recognize clearly from the time-faces of the gods that are put up for worship how dangerously archaic an hour European man keeps in Africa. We can tell from the time-face of his bearded tribal god that it is still the hour of an early Old Testament patriarch, not the hour of the reborn son but still of the unrealized father. And if we pause and reflect that since the vision of the reborn son, there has been also this delicate annunciation of woman in the spirit of man, this awareness of a re-creative feminine element in the masculine dominants of life and time which led the rough belted knights of Arthur on their quest, when you consider all that has happened in the human spirit since the angry days of Old Testament patriarchal unawareness, then you will realize how dangerously the "being" of my countrymen has receded in Africa, how wide is the gap between them and the time that contains their lives, and how obscure and unimagined are the ways in which real help can be given from the outside.

produce life, is feminine. England, again, is a mother country to the English and that fact, perhaps, helps to explain the undiminished vitality of the story of Hamlet in English imagination. Afrikaner South Africa is crystallizing rapidly as a father country and one of the foremost nationalist newspapers is called *Die Vaderland*.

QUESTION

You said in the beginning of your talk that it was as if the coming of the white man in the nineteenth century was a kind of answer to an unconscious hope of the black man in Africa. If I remember rightly you said you believed that it was only an assumption of this kind which could account for the comparative lack of violent physical conflict that was produced in Africa by the arrival of the white man. I find that a very interesting thought and I wonder if you have any other evidence for it?

ANSWER

Not other evidence, perhaps, but other ideas, and if you could promise to catch them as they fly and not bend them to yourselves I will tell you what they are!

You may know that since the coming of European man in Africa he has been confronted with a legend that somewhere in the heart of Africa resides a great and beautiful white queen. It is a curious legend and it exercises the imaginations of some white men almost as much as those of the articulate black man. Many of you no doubt will be familiar with the legend from the work of Rider Haggard, who significantly enough was one of the first to stare unknowingly at the reflection of his own hidden self and that of the Europe of his day in the mirror of darkest Africa. Now today we know Africa well enough to realize that no such queen exists and that probably no such queen has ever existed there. Nonetheless, the legend persists and it persists, I think, because it corresponds to a deep-seated need in the dreaming prophetic soul of man in Africa. If you believe as I do that the soul of man emerges from his hidden being as Aphrodite emerged from the foam and spray of a wine-red sea of morning and walks through his senses personified with magnetic beauty in the shape of a woman, you will understand why I find this legend of the beautiful white queen in Africa so significant. I think anyone who has really taken the trouble to know himself and his history will admit that there is, recognized or unrecognized, this compelling objective feminine presence in the spirit of man everywhere. It is demonstrated in the story of

the meeting of Dante and Beatrice and in the great
spiritual adventure that flowed from it. It is this
truth which gives Laura her meaning for Petrarch
and which is so movingly reflected in the legend of
Theseus and Ariadne. It is this feminine presence in
the spirit of man that spins the golden thread which
leads him back from battle with the Cretan monster
in the labyrinthine deeps of himself, and from her
comes the beauty that transforms the beast in him.
Alas, it is this presence, too, which has been rewarded by man with centuries of neglect wherein
he has left woman and her special being weeping
like Ariadne on a rocky splinter of himself, the waters
of his forgetfulness and ingratitude rising like a sea
round her. Happily this feminine element today is
slowly emerging from the long shadow of an immemorial neglect into the light of our day and taking
a place of her own in the conscious values of man.
In my own country, however, she is still so dangerously submerged that her existence is not even sus-
pected. But known or unknown she is there, as this
legend of which I have just spoken suggests. This
intimation of her presence in the African soul was
there long before the white man came to Africa and
before the aboriginal of Africa even knew that white

beings existed. And to prove it I know a wonderful rock painting hundreds of miles from the sea in the wasteland of south-west Africa. This painting is on a rock in a deep gorge surrounded by a great thirst-land which to this day is practically inaccessible. One of the central figures in this painting is an elegant and most bewitching white lady. She is stepping down the smooth path of this great rock carrying a white lotus in her hand—incidentally the lotus does not grow in Africa. Heaven knows how old this rock painting is, for estimates vary from hundreds to some thousands of years, but in any case everybody is agreed that it was painted long before the coming of the white man in Africa. Somehow I find that one magical painting the evidence for which you are asking. Also I find this white lady on a rock evidence of the profound mythological force which is active in the heart of all living matter, giving our little lives their direction, meaning and fullness in time. To me it is gracious manifestation of this force which expresses itself, however unrecognized, through our recorded histories and which also is trying to make itself articulate in this conflict in Africa. Lord Acton, out of his great intuition, once said that "much of the history of the world is a burden on the memory and not an illumination of the soul." I would like to add that there is this other kind of history in our blood, too, this mythological dominant of history and time which will, if neglected and ignored, lead not only to no illumination of the human soul but to this terrible darkening of the eye which I called "Mata Kelap" and tried to describe for you in this discussion.

QUESTION

The idea of an historical dominant, of this mythological content of history, fascinates many of us and we wonder if the speaker could not usefully elaborate it. Could he not, for instance, make its relation to national character and destiny clearer?

ANSWER

I will do so gladly as far as I can, because it may help to sketch in the wider considerations that influence what I have been trying to say. Even so, I cannot stray from my particular theme and must be brief. Let us return, therefore, at once to the German parallel we have been following thus far. Let us take a myth nearer our own time than the archaic prototype that has been our model hitherto. Let us take the myth which expresses itself in the legend of Faust, a myth to my mind of greater significance and potential than the older one. Now Faust is essentially a German spirit. As the great Burckhardt pointed

out long before the World War began to rumble on European soil, Faust is profoundly and peculiarly a German myth, so much so that when the medieval doctor made his notorious choice he chose not merely for himself but for a nation. For me the vitality of the Faustian theme in German imagination is another clear manifestation of an inescapable mythological pattern in national history.*
Its undiminished existence at this profound level of the German pattern indeed has always given me hope that the choice of the medieval doctor was not final and that it and all that evolved from it may well prove to have been only the terrible preliminaries to achieving on a national scale the transcendence described in the second half of Goethe's prophetic rendering of the legend. It always interests me, too, to remark how difficult it is to export the national myth from its native soil. Of course, the familiar myth has its following abroad as one would expect of a theme that went as deep into the life of a great people, but it is a very minor affair compared to its major orchestration at home. The English, for instance, have no particular need of the

* The distinguished German writer Thomas Mann not long ago was compelled to rearticulate the Faustian myth in a long novel in a contemporary setting.

Faustian legend. They have their own Elizabethan version of the myth but in comparison with the German model it is a boisterous, lyrical schoolboy affair. They are a more profoundly integrated people and this particular gap, this Faustian split, appears to be hermetically sealed in their national character. But that does not mean that they are immune to mythological visitations of history. They have other and equally dynamic myths. There is the myth, for example, expressed in their many legends of Arthur of the Round Table and the search of Arthur's company for the Holy Grail. However far you go back in the modern English spirit you will find that this myth contains and gives direction to it. To this day, for example, the concept of the knight still plays a part in the social machinery of their land. The English, too, have another, more pagan and archaic myth to trouble them—the myth of Hamlet. Hamlet is as English in spirit as Faust is German. Just as Hamlet continues to exercise the imagination of the English because it is rooted in a problem which has not yet been resolved for them, so the Faustian theme concerns a psychological conflict which remains real and active in the German soul to this very day. With my countrymen in Africa the German parallel is very close. It is true they have not achieved the articulation to express their own mythological urge in a personified form, but the choice to which their own inner development has brought them and which confronts them at this moment is also a Faustian choice. The conflict which rages within the spirit of my countrymen and which inspires their profound reaction and the reversion of their spirit to a more archaic pattern is this ancient conflict for the possession of the soul of individual man. Indeed, there is the constantly recurring situation in the history of man which, in the last analysis, is capable only of a religious solution. For religion is not religion unless it keeps burning bright in the dark hour the idea of life as a journey begun in the physical world and continued on into another world of "becoming." Religion is not religion unless it heals the dividing wound inflicted between these two levels of being and becoming. If the devil rules man by dividing himself against himself, God rules by uniting us within ourselves.

If, therefore, you accept that the problem which the *being* of European man creates in Africa is delivered and provoked in this religious dimension you may feel even more hopeless about it than before, for almost everywhere one sees a breakdown in the religious machinery of man, and you will find their churches failing my Afrikaner countrymen by widening the very division they were designed to heal and make whole in man. Nevertheless, I myself do not feel entirely hopeless about it. First, I know the potential heroic capacity of my countrymen as you could not be expected to know it, and I still have faith in the power of the myth which brought my countrymen to Africa and compelled them to set out on their great journey into the interior. Even to this day the imaginations and spirit of my countrymen revolve round the Great Trek with an obstinacy and intensity which is not capable of easy rational explanation. Their imaginations are still obsessed with this passage in their history as the spirit is obsessed only by visions that have not yet reached their end, and I am certain that the seed of suspicion is already planted in their hearts that the great journey of their forefathers must have another meaning beyond the surface values of their recorded histories.

QUESTION

You seem to have a great faith in this "sense of a
journey" within us. Is it not perhaps excessive? If
not, could you say why?

ANSWER

Well, to start with I believe the "sense of a
journey" and the "sense of a choice of ways" are
two constants in mythology and that fact alone
strikes me as important. Then I believe that this
sense of the journey goes very deep in all of us
whether we know it or not, though it is perhaps
more difficult for Europeans to understand than it is
for me. Long before man became a peasant he was
a nomad following the seasons across the ends of the
earth. I believe there was a time when man's capacity to journey was as vital to him as the air he
breathed and the food he ate, and that whole indigenous races of men have perished because foreign civilizations put an end to their freedom of

181

movement. I know a wise Australian who assured
me once that one of the main reasons why the
Australian aborigines, whom he had loved, had practically died out was because the freedom of their
unpredictable "walk-abouts" was so abruptly re-
stricted by the impositions of civilization. I myself
know another aboriginal race, the pygmy bushmen
of Africa, who are nomads and commit themselves
with unquestioning trust to travel round the desert
with the seasons, withstanding unimaginable hard-
ships. But let them commit one social offence and
get taken into civilized custody and they will pine
away. I knew of one who died within a few weeks
of incarceration for no reason except that the cur-
tailment of freedom of movement was the end of life
for him. So for these and many other reasons I believe that this "sense of a journey" within us com-
mands the most profound, powerful and creative
energies of man. I believe that the myth which provokes man to a journey flows directly from the unfailing source of life's transcendent aim and today
is concerned just as vitally with man's spiritual survival as it once was with his physical survival. But
of course it is obvious that in order to travel on with
this inner "sense of the journey" we need a new kind

of explorer, a new kind of pathfinder, human beings who, now that the physical world is spread out before us like an open book with the latest geographical mystery solved and the highest mountain climbed, are ready to turn and explore in a new dimension. And it is the myth, I believe, that gives us our first clue as to the way into this new-old dimension. That is why it is so important for us to endeavour to relearn its forgotten language so that we can understand its full meaning and relate it to our contemporary selves.

QUESTION

I like the speaker's idea of a new kind of explorer in an undiscovered dimension. But I still do not see sufficiently what he means. For instance, how can these new individuals set about their task?

ANSWER

To begin where your question ends, I would answer, by first becoming aware of the need and the response to the need implicit in the myth. Now that is increasingly happening. I mentioned earlier on that I am frequently struck by the numbers of individuals who no longer feel contained in their national and social context. Already there seems to me to be in existence a new kind of human being who is living ahead of the meaning of our time, knowing only that meaning has to be lived before it can be known, and that every step of the exacting journey has to be accomplished before new being can be discovered. Already in the world there are

many individuals who are so strongly attacked by
this need of contemporary reality that they experience the inadequacies of their communities as a
sickness of their own physical being. I know Germans who have died purely because of the sickness
of the pre-war German spirit. I know Frenchmen
today who are sick to death of the plague of rational
materialism of France. I knew many Japanese who
lost the will to live because of the refusal of their
nation to acknowledge the urge to new individual
being in its midst. I know many of my own countrymen, too, who are gravely ill in the same way. They
ail and die because the spirit of man is everlastingly
aboriginal and, like the Australian blackamoor, cannot do without its "walk-abouts" from the arrested
moments of its conscious self into the greater mean-
ings which surround it. The spirit of man is nomad,
his blood Bedouin, his being is frontiersman, and
only death possesses the right to bring to an end the
journey to which his myth provokes him. But already I believe many of these ailing individuals, imprisoned in an arrested moment of the history of
their nations, are beginning to discover the meaning
of their isolation and suffering. They are beginning
to discover that the sickness in them is not their

proper, individual affliction but belongs to a dying aspect of their cultures, communities, classes or races. Death is not theirs but rather that of the coward context that will not expand to become its journeying 1954 self. And in case this sounds over-fanciful I can give you an example from my own experience. We had a war in South Africa at the beginning of this century which we felt to be a cruel and unjust war and wherein we were defeated by the British. I was born four years after that war, yet war went on raging inside me right through my adolescence. I laboured under it as an individual sense of defeat in my heart that made it quite impossible for me to be my normal adventurous, forward-moving young self. I cannot tell you how my life was conditioned to this dreary automatic reflex of defeat and how ill it made me at times until one day I realized that it was an improper invasion of the past into my own urgent being. The moment I recognized this invason for what it was I was able to banish its foreign content from my life. Now I have a feeling that the same sort of thing is going on all over the world in a bigger way. Many individuals are finding they have been so busy living history that they were not living their "now" at all.

With a subsonic tremor of new music and a rever-
beration of the feet of the new community in their
ears, they then discover themselves becoming whole
directly they refuse to remain identified with the
sick and dying aspects of their societies. This process is going on also in Africa. I confess it is much
more retarded there, but it is in being. The desperate
problem there is to reverse, before it is too late, the
trend of the basic myth of my people. For, as I hope
I have made clear, there is nothing wrong with the
basic myth of my people. If instead of believing that
they are the *only* chosen people they could believe
that we are all chosen people charged in our unique
and several ways to bring the journey to its contracted end, our differences honourable, equal in
dignity and adding to the variety and wonder of life,
then all could be well. And a few people do realize
this. Perhaps one individual example of what I mean
would be helpful. Two years ago, the son of a
former governor-general of South Africa defied a
police order forbidding him to demonstrate in an
African area of Johannesburg. He was arrested as he
walked quietly into the area, tried and sentenced to
prison. Although I myself believe you can only
change a people truly by changing, not breaking,

their laws, by changing, not confusing, such order
as they have in their lives, I have always regarded
his action as inspired by real moral imagination and
as being the kind of deed that stirs the earth for the
first tender seedbed of the greater change of heart
that has to come. For consider precisely what he
did. He demonstrated in the unambiguous terms of
a living example that the conflict in South Africa
is not a conflict between white and black alone but
also, and more desperately still, a conflict between
white and white. He tried, as it were, to change the
gear of the living myth from reverse into first gear
and check its recession. And to check the recession
of our myths is, I believe, one of the most urgent
tasks of contemporary man, not to do away with
them, but to lend them the light of our reason and
intellect, for we all need our myths constantly and
forever. Does not Cervantes' *Don Quixote* most movingly symbolize just this truth? The knight of La
Mancha and his peasant follower ride on in all of
us from our first classic rose-pink dawn to our last
romantic twilight. For the knight and the peasant
are not two separate people, but one; the knight
riding in search of a fit cause for his dedicated and
heroic spirit is symbol of the aboriginal myth in us

seeking flesh and blood to make it a living reality; the peasant following grumbling behind is our physical worldly self which clings to the myth, for without its spirit his life has no meaning. They are two aspects of one continuing and ambivalent truth: without nations and communities the myth cannot live; but without myth the life of a people lacks direction and meaning. Tragedy comes when one or other of these inseparable aspects is made to usurp the validity of the other and to masquerade as the totality, as, for instance, when the knight rejects the evidence of the peasant's vision in a worldly issue and attacks shepherds and sheep as robbers. Yet there is no disaster so great as when the spirit is denied its journey—when the knight loses his horse, spear and cause—for when that happens a terrible meaninglessness invades life. We have only to look round us to see how high a tide of meaninglessness has already arisen in the being of man, and how denied is his legitimate meaning in the society to which he belongs. He has been driven more and more to rediscover it illegitimately through social upheaval and war. I believe this growing desperation is largely because the institutions and societies of our day will not give their constituent members

causes worthy of their heroic capacities and love.
Society treats men as children that must not be exposed to risk and insecurity, or to revert to my basic
image, it refuses the knight his armour, his horse
and his cause and separates him from his peasant.*
This subterranean mood exists also in Africa. Yet
what is needed there is not to destroy its myths but
rather to prevent their regression and archaic pro-
liferation, to bring them up into the light of day and
give them all their full contemporary meaning. In
that meaning I am certain there is room for com-

---

* Nations appear to me to have the same sort of problem with
their history, and the individual with his community, as children
have with their parents. There are retarded nations who go on
hiding behind their history just as a nervous child hides behind
the skirts of its mother. They use history as a justification for
shirking their own proper responsibilities in the present and
getting others to carry their burden for them, or they become
overassertive and, under cover of history, snatch what is not
theirs at all. The way a generation of my country who never
fought in it continues half a century after to hide behind the
Boer War is an illustration in point. Indeed, the parallel between
the state of mind of the modern problem child and modern nationalism, for instance, has always impressed me. Nationalism
so often seems to me the juvenile delinquency of the contemporary world. Nations do not seem to become grown-up until they
leave their history behind them like a young man going out into
the world for the first time to earn a living and rights of his own,
accepting the consequences of the past as his own immediate
problem in its own immediate setting. Similarly, it seems to me
that an individual is not mature until he ceases to shelter behind his community, honours it by speaking his mind openly to it
and walking upright before it in a way of his own.

munity of spirit for all races and colours in Africa. But there can be no magical solution. The answer will have to be lived, humbly and painfully, from beginning to end at all levels. Unfortunately the Western world can be so arrogant in its thinking that it suffers from the illusion that one can deal with these great problems merely by thinking out a proper solution and then putting it into effect through logical alterations in the political and social machinery of man. Nothing as superficial as that can happen without disaster, least of all in Africa. The individual must instead endeavour to synchronize the basic myth of his people to its desperate native hour and so bring back the submerged creative energies of the myth into the hurt and confused field of his native continent. Luckily, I believe, there are a great and growing number of my people who are determined to prevent Africa from repeating the pattern of disaster with which history, both here and in the East, has made us so familiar, believing that thereby Africa may save not only itself but also the rest of the world.

QUESTION

I am a South African studying in Europe and I have
been horrified by the extremely distorted view
people in Europe have of events in South Africa. I
must be frank and say that I do not find what you
have said tonight very helpful. But I am grateful
for what you have just said about not destroying
what you call "the myth" in South Africa, for that
seems to indicate that you may believe that it is
right to preserve white civilization in Africa. Is
this so?

ANSWER

Of course I believe in white civilization, using
white in the inner sense defined before. I believe in
the increase of Western civilization and its preservation in Africa because I believe most profoundly in
the increase of consciousness. So much do I believe
in it that I feel sure that whatever form of life we
achieve in Africa must be by the hard way of a
deeper and expanding awareness of ourselves, our
being and the meaning of life, rather than by a re-

cession into the unconscious state from which mankind has so slowly and so painfully risen. I think the great danger in Africa arises from the fact that we are not aware enough of our meaning, vocation and purpose there. Our "consciousness" is fanatically narrow and has incurred tremendous instinctive enmities by its bigoted rejection and obstinate refusal to recognize other forces and values in the nature of man. It is not that we want to sacrifice the reason and intellect to which our culture owes so much, but we must oppose the presumptions of reason and intellect—their wilful refusal to cooperate, and their insistence on dominating other valid aspects of the spirit of man. I believe that no matter what solution we arrive at in Africa it must be preceded by an enormous expansion of the awareness of modern man in Africa, an expansion that will allow all the rich instinctive values which play so great a part in the life of the black man round us also to play a legitimate role in our own lives inevitably expressing itself in a liberalization of our own institutions and a broadening of the relationships between its human constituent members. In that sense I believe most profoundly in the preservation of white civilization in Africa.

QUESTION

You seem to me still to be evading the real issue.
Would you please tell me whether you would be
happy to see your son married to a black woman?
You need only say "yes" or "no."

ANSWER

Ask me any questions you like about Africa and I
will try to answer them, but I am not prepared for
you to tell me how I must answer them! So let us
begin by deciding what we mean by marriage, not
in the archaic, but in the 1954 sense. In the Western
world one has only to study the lengthening casualty
lists in the daily newspapers to realize that marriage
is one of the main battlegrounds of the spirit of the
age. Marriage, too, with the demands of our being,
has moved towards a more specific and conscious
state of reality. There was a time when marriage was
almost entirely contained in its biological and social
aspects. But today men and women are demanding

something more of marriage than that. The social
and biological aspects are still of profound primary
importance, but today men and women are less content to be only the begetters and the custodians of
one another's children. They are beginning to be
aware of the need for a more personal and individual relationship with one another and their communities. They have, therefore, a more exacting need
of one another's natures. It is all of a piece with our
present-day need for man to be more conscious and
take the burden of his being more fully upon himself. Woman, both in the mind of man and in the life
round us, has come out of the shadows of a purely
sociological function and is emerging more and more
as an individual with a conscious need and purpose
of her own just as valid as those of man, who, for so
long, has been the principal figure in the drama.
This new emerging concept of marriage, therefore,
is far more difficult and complex than the less conscious states which preceded it. With almost everything in its favour, differences of class, language and
religion can still wreck the success of the relationship, so, naturally, one would hesitate to add to
these difficulties further differences of race and
colour and the problems the world creates because

of these differences. I would not be happy if a son of mine were to marry somebody not of his own people who did not share his way of looking at life; but my unhappiness would have little to do with prejudice against the colour of the woman in question.

Mixed marriages, from what I have seen of them, do not lead to very happy results, but this may reflect more on our general world attitude to questions of colour than from difficulties in the union itself. I know a black woman who grew up in England and married an Englishman, and she has had a really inspired and inspiring relationship with her husband.

Then there is one other point I would like to mention. However unwise it may be at this stage in their development for white and black to marry, we should always remember that those who do so are perhaps doing something of far-reaching historical value by demonstrating that, at the deepest levels in human nature in the dimension of love, there can never be such a thing as colour prejudice. I am not suggesting that this would constitute a good reason for mixed marriages, for, again, I believe that marriage is something which human beings should contract for itself alone and for no other consideration whatsoever. Nevertheless, I think it is important that in considering these problems we should realize that the humble individuals, black and white, who have contracted a union in obedience to an urge of life in them, are perhaps unwittingly serving a cause both of history and life.

QUESTION

You spoke of the breakdown in the religious machinery of man. I am not aware that the Afrikaner churches have broken down. When I left South Africa to come and study here a year ago they were still full to overflowing on Sundays. I fail utterly to see how you can imply that they have lost contact with our people.

ANSWER

Thank you for your question. It is quite true that the Afrikaner churches have not lost contact with their community. I am amazed every time I go back —and I go back at least once a year—to see how they grow and expand in the physical world. Remote hamlets that had no church when I was a boy now have two, three and even four churches. Designing and building new churches for the Afrikaner people is a great, thriving and growing industry, and what is more, fast as the churches go up, they are never empty. In comparison with the churches of other communities they would appear on the surface to be in a most enviable position. But when you look deeper into the situation and examine what they preach in those churches you will find that they have kept contact with the people only at what I believe to be a frightening sacrifice of religion. They have kept contact not by drawing their community after them on this journey of "becoming" which we have discussed at some length, but by turning back and perilously reversing their step in an amply discredited direction. They have remained popular at the price of going down into their people and playing a political rather than a religious role. At times it is even difficult to tell which is the more powerful, an early form of ancestor worship or Old Testament worship. Levy Bruhl said, "The dream is the real god of primitive people." The South African people carrying their churches with them have receded to a point in their spirit where a racial myth, a racial dream of history, is their real God. That explains the ease with which Afrikaner priests go from the pulpit into politics; there is at heart no longer any serious difference of level between the two: both

serve the same master. Even if you do not, I consider what is happening to be a most serious breakdown in the religious machinery of my country. I
go further, I call the process a betrayal of the religious urge which originally brought us to Africa.

QUESTION

When I listen to you I cannot believe that you are a true South African, but I hope all the same you will allow me one more question. You mentioned a head of state who said that the "true task of a university was to serve the state." Would you please give us his name and the name of those whom you hold primarily responsible for this state of affairs in Africa?

ANSWER

I could answer easily but you must forgive me if I decline to do so. Aristotle once said that if the human mind wanted the right answers it must first learn to formulate the right questions. Your question, I fear, is not such a one and I will tell you why. The situation we are discussing in Africa is not caused by any particular individual. It is caused by all of us and by what we each are not only publicly but also in the privacy of our lives. I wish it were not so, for then it would be possible to solve the problem merely by removing from power certain individuals. But unfortunately this is not the situation at all. It is what I would call a mythical or herd situation and is not consciously created and controlled by individuals. It is a situation wherein the conscious resistance of individual units is gradually being invaded and slowly being drawn out to sea on an ebb tide in the blood of a whole people. In countries going through this kind of experience, if you remove by force the entire government in power they will only be replaced on the morrow by exactly the same kind of people, for in these situations the so-called leaders do not control what they lead, they merely express and follow a negative unconscious trend which has possessed the spirit of their people. You need not be in South Africa long before becoming aware of this. Everywhere there is a stifling emanation of a compulsive racial mystique which underlines the lovely light of Africa with long blue-pencil shadows. You have only to speak to the people to be aware of this irrational obsession and to realize sadly that they are in a deep dungeon of themselves beyond the reach of any rational communication. I say this to you with some assurance because I have had some personal experience of these atmospheric conditions in other nations. In Japan long before the war happened in the physical world, I felt it already in being, weighing on the spirit of the Japanese people and in the minds of my Japanese friends, beating the air about them like the wings of one of their mythical dragons. I felt it over and over again in pre-Nazi Germany and once again after the war in the upsurgent countries of South East Asia. I believe the same process is now at work in Africa and equally I assure you that at this phase of its development, it has little to do with mass leaders and leadership. One day, perhaps, the nations of the world will recognize this and take it into greater account in their reckonings for the future and behaviour in the present.

QUESTION

I am an Englishwoman and I wonder if there is any
way in which we in England can help you with this
very great problem in Africa? Is there anything specific that we can do to help to overcome these awful
tensions, say in Kenya or South Africa, which you
have described to us tonight?

ANSWER

How can one ever pass on what one imagines to
be one's own experience of what is true and helpful
to other human beings who are in need of it? I am
not sure to what extent it is possible; but I am sure
that it is possible only by example. So already in a
great many ways the people in Britain have helped
us in Africa by reason of what they have achieved
in their own society and institutions and by the
quality of their being. There are other ways, too, of
helping, though they are perhaps more negative
than positive.

First, you must not allow yourselves to hate us in Africa. That is important. Slowly but surely people in Britain are beginning to despise and hate the white man and evaluate the black and coloured man in Africa in a way that is neither real nor true. You are beginning to believe that in Africa the white man, particularly the Afrikaner, is a new kind of de- praved human monster unworthy of sympathy and love. You are beginning to regard the wrong that he does as an unnatural wrong, his sins as sins that are not like those of other men, particularly not like your own and therefore deserving of a severity of judg- ment and censure which you do not apply in your own affairs. You tend to deny our errors in Africa the excuse of human fallibility and subject my coun- tryman to inhuman condemnations. You are thereby hastening what is most to be feared: the inhumani- zation and impersonalization of the problem. It is true a great many of my countrymen in South Africa are behaving in the most deplorable way, which, if not corrected, will lead them straight to disaster. Yet they are not to be hated for that. The difficulties that beset a minority civilization in such a vast primi- tive context as Africa are real in a way which Euro- peans cannot adequately understand. It may be true

that power corrupts but no power corrupts so subtly
as civilized power in a helpless primitive world.
Nor must you forget that there are thousands of
people in Africa who sincerely believe they are following the only course open to them. I think, therefore, that it is of the utmost importance to acknowledge this feeling of rightness and to recognize that
in the meaning men give to their actions (however
deplorable their actions may be) lies the key to re-
leasing their spirit for a different level. If there is
a form of theft lower than thieving itself, it is to rob
the thief of such little honour as he possesses, for
by so doing you deny him the opportunity of dis-
covering the real meaning of his actions and de-
prive him of the one thing through which he can
be redeemed from thieving. Similarly, you in Great
Britain can help by trying to find out with us in
Africa today the meaning of this misguided "right"
which is expressing itself in this conflict. The worst
thing that anyone can do in these circumstances is
to add to the race or individual's sense of ostracism.
Surely the best doctors are those who have no horror
but almost a love of the maladies and plagues
against which they pit themselves? The best priests,
too, are not those who are horrified by sin, but those

for whom sin confirms the warm, searching, inde-
fatigable humanity of the sinners in their charge.
Unfortunately one of the worst effects of our excessive Protestant development has been our growing
intolerance of one another's sins and therefore our
increasing incomprehension of the meaning of sin.
The European in Africa cannot be punished or
hated into being a better person. If you could endeavour to understand this painful segment of unrealized time in their spirit which I have tried to
describe to you, and try to prevent yourselves from
taking sides in the battle that rages in Africa, urging
only that its solution shall come out of all the
peoples, races and colours of Africa and not out of
any particular section of them, then you would help
us a great deal. For the only sane concept of society
is one wherein the constituent interests cannot possibly diverge, and where the interest of the whole is
resolutely defended against anyone or anything that
would splinter it apart. Switzerland is an example of
what I mean.

But there is yet another contribution that you in
Britain can make towards this difficulty in Africa.
Refuse to work off on Africa the moral ardour which
you need for your own lives in Europe. Prevent

yourselves from projecting this deep conflict which rages also in the spirit of modern man in Europe onto us in Africa. One complication of the whole situation is that Africa is a kind of vast Greek theatre for the modern world wherein you see performed, in its most dramatic and romantic form, the ancient conflict of man and the fate that is within him. The black man and the white man in Africa, primitive natural man and civilized synthetic man in Africa, personify two ancient aspects of man that are continually at war in the heart of the individual. The onlooker of this vast drama in Africa, therefore, like the baboon with the mirror, is apt to mistake the conflict without for the conflict which rages within himself and to imagine that by taking sides in Africa he is really helping to solve the problem. I can only explain this by suggesting that nations as well as individuals project their own problems onto the lives and situations of their neighbours, and you in Britain, most subtly, tend to do the same thing to us. You have a tendency to expect of us in Africa a standard of morality which you have not always realized in your own country. Let me give you an example. Several years ago I was discussing, with some of your leaders, this tendency of the political parties in Britain to project what are essentially British political tensions into the scene in Africa. As I was talking one of them interrupted by saying, "Well you see, Colonel, I am only a simple miner, but when I go out to Africa and discover that the white miners there will not allow the black miners into their unions I find it very wrong and cannot stomach it."

I answered, "I agree with you that such a situation does exist in Africa and is wrong. But let us be absolutely fair in this matter. At the present time in Britain you have a grievous shortage of both miners and coal. Mr. Bevin has just pleaded, saying, 'give me more coal and I can follow a more independent foreign policy in the world.' Yet, at this very moment your miners in Britain have refused at any price to take in Italian miners to work with them. Surely this is a clear example of how often you expect from Africa a standard of conduct which you are unable to achieve in your own country?"

Yet this game of being high-minded at other people's expense is being played out night and day with disastrous effects in the world. If you can stop yourselves from doing this to us in Africa and so add to the energies you need for your own problems you will help us a great deal. If you could, for instance, solve all these class, religious and national prejudices that make Europe one of the bloodiest battlegrounds in the history of mankind and give us a truly united and integrated Western Europe, you will have helped us in Africa more than I can say.

QUESTION

I am an American and I have been deeply moved by what I have heard. Like the lady whose question has just been answered, I too want to ask what we can do to help. I realize that much of what has been said to her would apply also to us, but I wonder if there is not a peculiarly American angle to this problem which has not been touched on yet and whether Colonel van der Post could not briefly say something about it.

ANSWER

Yes, there is. You know I always think of this problem in layers. I think of it first and most keenly in the South-African layer at the quick of myself. I think of it next in its African layer, then the layers in relation to Britain and Europe, America, the Near East and Far East, and so on. I must confess that the American angle, as you call it, has an importance in my mind almost as great as the British and European one. I do not know even whether angle is not the wrong word and whether parallel would not be a more accurate one. I'll try and tell you why not without diffidence for I have never been to America. I can speak only from what I have read of your country and know of your literature and art. But like us, it seems to me, you are people today mainly of uprooted and transplanted European stock. Your forefathers, too, were dumped in a great primitive world, new only in the most superficial sense but in all others old and drenched with time. They too, so it seems to me, were slowly but surely forced by the post-Reformation tide in the European spirit into a pitiless struggle with primitive America. All I know of your history suggests to me that unseen in the shadow of your reasoning spirit, the same sort of dividing mechanism I now know so well in Africa was relentlessly at work setting you and the Red Indian at one another's throats. If that were not so, I believe you would have found a bridge long since over the gulf which divided you so cruelly from the natural children of your great land. I see you consciously maintaining this rejection of primitive America with a rare, frantic and even heroic stubbornness. Yet despite your conscious stand, I see the

land of America bending your nature to its own
secret will and transforming you into a people that
is not European any more. You yourselves acknowledge the change by calling yourselves American as
we do a similar transformation in Africa by calling
ourselves Afrikaners, but I often wonder to what
extent you are really aware of how deep the change
goes and how vital is the challenge it throws out to
your spirit or whether like us in Africa you do not
still tend to see it as just another sociological and
political variant in the Western scheme of things.
I'll tell you why I wonder this in a minute; the
more immediate point is that in your initial rejection
of the primitive and more natural life of America, I
see your parallel as very close to ours. But there is
something else which brings it closer still. You have
in the course of your development taken primitive
Africa into your midst. You have added to the diminishing primitive content of your land by borrow-
ing lavishly from the great primitive treasure-house
of Africa. As a result today there is a large tract of
your spirit which is also African whether you like it
or not, whether you know it or not. I continually
hear the great undertones of this other American-
Africa in your music and see its rhythms in your

dancing and your art. In this process of bringing Africa to America you have run the danger of rejecting and invalidating the primitive a second time and the factor which creates the prejudices of mind and heart that constitute that danger, I believe, is the same as ours. The example you set in overcoming these prejudices, therefore, cannot escape having the most resounding consequences in Africa and indeed the rest of the world. Please do not think that when I talk of the danger of a second rejection of the primitive in your society as still existing that I am ignorant of what you have done in your legislation and history to honour the African in your midst and the terrible civil war you fought to bring about his liberation in your society. I know these things and they clearly have an importance that cannot be overlooked or underrated. But they are only one dimension of the problem. The root goes deep into each of you as it does into each of us in Africa; the civil war has vanished from the scene into the wings of history only to go, unseen and unrecognized, raging on over the same issues in the heart and mind of the individual. It is there that an honourable peace must first be achieved before the danger will vanish from your land, mine and the rest of the world. Let

us make no mistake about it; this is a world issue.
It is the most urgent issue of our desperate age and
it needs a dedicated attention to its origins in the
invisible soil of our inmost selves if it is not to end
in world disaster. I spoke to you earlier on of this
dark child of nature, this other primitive man within
each of us with whom we are at war in our spirit;
one of the causes we are so blindly at war is because
we cannot understand what he is trying to say to us.
There is a whole natural language of the spirit that
we have lost and can no longer receive or read. It
is what I called the aboriginal language of the spirit.
If we could only obtain access to it again and learn
to read its hieroglyphic script anew in the silence
of our hearts, the barbarisms of mind that have produced such terrible wars in our societies, would be
revealed to us and be bought back to their lawful
proportions. I believe one way to rediscovering that
language is for us to honour the primitive man in
our societies, not to reject him any longer, but to
lend him the light of our own reason and the shelter
of our own conscious knowledge. One way is for us
to go not to teach but to sit down humbly beside him
and patiently listen to this natural language speaking in his natural spirit and learn to translate it into

our own. I said I wondered if you realized how great a challenge this change of the European into American threw out to you. I wondered because if you did I imagine you would already be following this way; you would be going not in single specialist spies but in battalions to the reserves of your vanishing Indian, to beg his pardon and patiently beseech him to reveal to you the vital pattern that your great and teeming earth has made in his spirit. Yes, you would go to your first authentic and almost vanished American not to teach but to learn just as we in Africa would go to the Bushmen in the Kalahari and relearn from them this lost language of the spirit, the secret of recommunion with the rejected half of our life and of wholeness with our sacred mother earth, if pride of reason and excess of humanity had not turned our hearts to stone. Learning to do that with them one day, we should also be learning perhaps to do that to our inmost selves and resolution would come to our conflict at last, so that it might also come to the world. Only in order to do that we must humble our daily practical and rational selves who scorn this way, who cannot see the riches and magic behind the squalor and the dirt and the dust wherein so much of the primitive world has been confined and cannot accept that man must learn also from what he so abhors and rejects. It, too, is part of the great secret which Christ tried to pass on to us when he spoke of the stone which the builders rejected becoming the cornerstone of the building to come. "The cornerstone" of this new building of a warless nonracial world, I believe, must be those races and those aspects of life which we have despised and rejected for so long. You and we have acquired great power in the physical world. Our adventure in the physical world I am certain is far from over, but before we can go on further with it without disaster we must match it with greater understanding of ourselves and our natures. You have an America, we an Africa within us on whose merest thresholds we are standing. Not until we have travelled and known those great continents within as we have travelled and know them without, shall we be ready for our next great physical adventure which I truly believe will be to the stars. If you could show us this humble way I do not see how we could fail.

Author's Note

Colonel David Stirling, DSO, to whom this book is dedicated, is a member of an ancient, aristocratic Highland family from the highlands of Scotland. In fact, David himself was one of the gentlemen ushers in Westminster Abbey at the time of the coronation of the Queen. But he is known throughout Britain and the British Empire for the extremely original and valorous part he played in the war. He entered the war as a subaltern in the Scots Guards—he is only thirty-eight today—and was sent out with the famous Eighth Army to North Africa. There he quickly formed his own ideas about how the German-Italian lines of supply could be most effectively harassed at a moment when we were in a desperate and heavily outnumbered situation. Like everything else he does, he no sooner was convinced of the rightness of his ideas than he went straight to the High Command and put his ideas to them with such persuasion that he was given authority to proceed. He thereupon formed the long range Desert Reconnaissance Group and became one of the most formidable thorns in the Germans' flesh. He was captured by them much later in the war during a raid which suddenly descended from out of the Sahara Desert, hundreds of miles behind the front lines.

He is a person of immense physical and moral courage and the stories of his courageous behaviour, as courageous in prison as in the battlefield, are many and legendary. While in prison, he thought very long and deeply about the problems of Africa and, curiously enough, came quite independently to the same conclusions I had come to years before in my own native Africa. I was developing these in another prison, after being caught by the Japanese for trying to harry them in their lines of communication through the jungles of Java and Sumatra.

After the war, David went out to Africa to try to start a business career of his own, but he wasn't long there before he realized that there was something far more important to be done in Africa than business. He realized that unless the white man in Africa could be made to overcome the prejudices which di-

vide him from the black man and make him such a
bad controller of the black man's destiny, the European society would speedily crumble and vanish
from the continent of Africa. What is more, he realized that unless both white and black could produce
an idea in Africa which would harness their emotions and imaginations in a common effort, a period
of disaster lay ahead. So he and several others who
felt as he did formed what is now called the Society
of Capricorn. It is called that because it is concerned
principally, for the moment, with the area of British
Africa which lies north of the Tropic of Capricorn—
that is, between Capricorn and Cancer.

The aim of this society is to remove all these base
prejudices from the life of Capricorn Africa and to
provide both the black and the white man with a
common transcendent purpose. The society did not
spring from the heads of its founders into the world
fully armed like Pallas Athene from the head of
Zeus, but it has slowly and quietly, without seeking
publicity, studied its problems and prepared itself
for launching the great campaign to make partner-
ship in Africa between all civilized men of whatever
race and colour a lasting reality. What is unique
about it is that for the first time it is a movement in

this direction that has not been imposed on Africa from the outside, but is deeply rooted in Africa within. Already, for some years, Africans and Indians and white men who are members of this society have been sitting side by side planning how this great work is to be done. Very soon now, Africa and the world will be informed more fully of how Capricorn and its members intend to do this unique pioneering work in Africa.